the southern cottage

from THE BLUE RIDGE MOUNTAINS
to THE FLORIDA KEYS

the southern cottage

from THE BLUE RIDGE MOUNTAINS
to THE FLORIDA KEYS

text and photographs by
SUSAN SULLY

RIZZOLI
NEW YORK

THIS BOOK IS DEDICATED to the keepers of cottages—both to the protectors of charming houses that have provided hospitality and pleasure to generations of southerners, and to the builders of new ones that honor the lessons of these lovely old houses.

THIS BOOK IS ALSO DEDICATED to the memory of Gayle Fenning, whose spirit dwells in a dear old cottage home in the hearts of all who knew her.

First published in the United States of America in 2007 by Rizzoli International Publications, Inc.
300 Park Avenue South, New York, NY 10010
www.rizzoliusa.com

Text and photography copyright © 2007 Susan Sully

2007 2008 2009 2010 / 10 9 8 7 6 5 4 3 2 1

Printed in China

ISBN-10: 0-8478-2919-7
ISBN-13: 978-0-8478-2919-4
Library of Congress Control Number: 2006939427

Project Editor: Sandra Gilbert

Designed by Element Group

Credits:
Home by the Sea, by A. P. Carter, © 1978, Peer International Corporation, used by permission, all rights reserved.

Frontispiece: *Traditional Shingle-style details add pristine beauty to this renovated early-twentieth-century beach cottage in Virginia Beach, Virginia.*

Above: *An arched trellis forms a gateway linking the Cornwells' cottage garden with the sylvan landscape beyond in Flat Rock, North Carolina.*

Page 7: *Porch-ceiling blue shutters and an old-fashioned screened door lend cottage charm to this outbuilding at Shadowland, a historic Arts and Crafts cottage in Troutville, Virginia.*

Pages 16–17: *Time-darkened Shingle-style cottages known as the Unpainted Aristocracy line a stretch of beach at Nag's Head, North Carolina.*

Pages 126–127: *This corner of the porch overlooking the lake is a favorite gathering spot, not only for the Cornwells and their guests, but also for hummingbirds and butterflies.*

Table of Contents

introduction

southern shores

country retreats

There's a lonely cottage by the sea side
Where the water lilies strew the shore
It was there I passed my happy childhood
With a loved one that's gone before

Then give me back my dear old home
That old home by the sea
And I never will wander far away
From my home my dear old cottage home . . .

Many years have passed since there I wandered
But the old cot ne're has been forgot
And my heart in fancy oft returns
To that dear old familiar spot

Yes my heart is like the humming sea shell
That tells of its birth where e're it roams
I will sing of my cottage by the sea shore
Of my home my dear old cottage home

HOME BY THE SEA
written by A. P. Carter
and first recorded by the Carter Family in 1933

the spirit of the southern cottage

Southerners have a long tradition of building cottage getaways along the coast, in the mountains, or in remote woodland glades. In part, this tradition was spawned by seemingly endless summers, when heat and humidity make flight to cooler, airier realms a practical necessity. This was certainly true in the days before electricity and air conditioning, when the hope of catching a cooling breeze in an urban home was vain. Although eighteenth- and nineteenth-century city houses were designed to function as well as possible in the South's semitropical and tropical climates, they could not provide adequate respite from the elements in the dead heat of summer. Even plantation homes, with their large rooms, high ceilings, commodious porches, and center halls designed to invite ventilation, were considered not only uncomfortable but even unhealthy in the summer months.

In the days before modern medicine, miasma—damp air rising from swamps, mud flats, and riverbanks—was considered the cause of deadly infections from yellow fever and malaria. In fact, it was the mosquitoes that thrive in such still, damp conditions that spread the feared diseases, so southerners were right when they chose to remove to breezy ocean spots or mountain destinations during the summer months. Packing a season's worth of clothing,

A table of cut-tile mosaic from Fez adds a note of the exotic to Susan and Trenholm Walker's screened porch, which serves as an outdoor dining and living room. Antique painted metal benches from France, adorned with pillows, provide a comfortable perch from which to enjoy the garden.

possessions, and paraphernalia, they decamped to second homes along the shores or in higher altitudes in late May or early June.

"Anyone with two nickels to rub together would leave Charleston in the summer," I once heard Emily Whaley, author of *Mrs. Whaley and Her Charleston Garden*, say. Having endured several Charleston summers, even with the aid of air conditioning, I understand the conviction with which she uttered these words. After visiting her summer home in Flat Rock, North Carolina (now the second home of her daughter, Marty Whaley Adams Cornwell, and featured in this book), I realized that the southern cottage is not just about escape, but also arrival at an enchanted destination. For the charm of the southern cottage lies not simply in what it is not—a sweltering city house—but also what it is: a cherished place for leisure.

If the primary purpose of a southern cottage is practical necessity, a secondary impulse that informs it is a highly refined sense of leisure. There is something about the southerner that understands the immeasurable value derived from a few hours sitting idly upon a porch and taking in the surroundings or telling well-embroidered tales. And certainly, southerners love holing up with extended families or visiting with neighbors for hours, or even days, on end. Perhaps this is why they often emigrated en masse to summer spots like Flat Rock and the Outer Banks of North Carolina, or Georgia's Tybee Island; it was not enough to flee the heat—they had to create a seasonal society.

In the nineteenth century, the southern resorts that flourished along the coast and in the mountains boasted not only healthy environs but also a heady round of social activity. Ballrooms and dancing pavilions were typical amenities of seaside and mountain hotels such

as Asheville's Grove Park Inn and Virginia Beach's Cavalier, where southerners practiced their social graces during the summer season. This love of social gatherings extended to the home as well. Many southern cottages feature large parlors and dining rooms that can accommodate seasonal fêtes, thus defying the assumption that a cottage is a diminutive dwelling of casual charm.

However, in keeping with the relaxed rural atmosphere, these at-home entertainments were typically devoid of the formality required of city parties. The women wore simple frocks of muslin and the men, cool suits of linen and seersucker. Decorations consisted chiefly of the wildflowers that grew in profusion and Japanese lanterns. Comestibles were made of the summer bounty: simple tomato sandwiches or dressed shellfish. And guests were drawn from the community of neighbors and relations nearby. Such practices still flourish in summer cottages today, where tomato sandwiches or crab salad are produced for guests without the slightest effort, along with gallons of mint-garnished iced tea and lemonade.

Other southern cottages offered leisure of a different sort, a place where society was hard to find and nature prevalent. This was an escape sought primarily by men fleeing the trappings of civilization for isolated fish camps or hunting cottages—rustic dwellings by the sea or in the woods where they might pursue more basic instincts, fishing, hunting, and swapping stories until daybreak. Such getaways are elemental cabins built from whatever materials were at hand, with no luxuries, but plenty of fresh air.

Today, like the beach cottages, these rustic getaways are enjoyed by all members of the family. Old seaside fish camps or hunting cabins in the mountains

A clawfooted iron tub and a metal garden chandelier furnish a tiny bathhouse beside an old Virginia Beach cottage.

Fashioned of bamboo grown nearby, this outdoor shower, tucked beneath dense vegetation, offers interior designer Amelia Handegan a delightful way to refresh after a walk or bike ride on Folly Beach, South Carolina.

have been transformed into equal-opportunity vacation homes, or have inspired contemporary counterparts. One of the cottages featured in this book is a new home in the Florida panhandle development of WaterColor, which architect Jim Strickland and his wife Linda decorated with the rustic charm of a fish camp. Another is an old log cabin where Lucy Tkachenko enjoys life on the banks of a Roanoke Valley creek in Virginia. Yet another is the honeymoon cottage of Susan and Trenholm Walker on the island of Wadmalaw, South Carolina, a traditional location for Charlestonians seeking a retreat from urban life.

Urbanites Morgan Delaney and Osborne Mackie find weekend respite in a simple farmhouse in the Virginia Hunt Country, where generations of Washingtonians have flocked for hunting and rural recreations. Floridians Jill and Mac Easton have left the city entirely to raise their family in a house adjacent to an old summer cottage in Atlantic Beach, Florida. And a South Carolina land developer and his family enjoy summer sojourns in a collection of antique cabins poised above a trout-stocked lake in Cashiers, North Carolina.

What is the allure today of these simple southern cottages for people who travel the world with ease and enjoy the benefits of modern architecture and air conditioning? It is the promise of a simpler life, in which one can fall to sleep lulled by the call of night birds, awake in the middle of the night to the murmur of the ocean or a creek, and enjoy cool mornings sipping coffee on a breezy porch. And it is about sharing these moments with family and friends.

Southern cottages, though often small, are all about hospitality: the ability to offer comfort and society to groups both large and small. "Five person per bed limit" read a sign once posted on the walls of the Butler family cottage on Florida's panhandle. The sign was put up in jest, but in reality, large gatherings of family members do pile into the house each summer. Author Josephine Humphreys remembers childhood summers in Sullivan's Island, South Carolina, when her extended family occupied a diminutive cottage. The house was knee-deep with relatives, and that was only half the fun. The other half was living in a cottage close by the sea (and sea breezes) with porches overlooking a natural landscape filled with possums and shorebirds.

The allure, then, of the southern cottage is one part natural setting (whether the ocean, creek, or woodlands), one part family togetherness (whether that means just two loving partners, or an extended family of twenty), and one part hospitality (offered to neighbors, visiting relations, or even complete strangers). It's about living close to nature, with plentiful windows and porches opening onto vistas and the scents and sounds of the environment. It's about spending time together, without the diversions of media rooms and urban entertainments. And it's about being present—to the sight of humming birds and herons returning from their seasonal migrations, to the sounds of the wind or the sea, and especially to the rhythms of life, whether the chatter of children or the breath of one's soul.

This is the spirit of the southern cottage. Welcome.

The sole of a child's shoe, studded with shells, is among the many objects that have washed ashore to find a place in Susan and Trenholm Walker's home.

Although individual southern cottages themselves are quite often diminutive, the overall subject of the southern cottage is huge and unwieldy. As I researched this book, I decided to narrow my field to cottages that were either built as, or have become, seasonal getaways. This decision meant leaving out many wonderful styles of urban cottages—New Orleans' Creole cottages, Charleston's freedman's cottages, the South's early-twentieth-century bungalows, and so on. I also decided to restrict the geographic scope of this volume to cottages in the southeastern states, purely because I found so many wonderful homes in this area that I had more than filled a book before moving further inland. In order to unify the contents, I limited myself to homes, both old and new, that reflect southern vernacular architectural styles and honor traditional southern cottage values of family togetherness, unpretentious style, and intimacy with their surroundings.

I hope this book will inspire readers who are thinking about restoring an old southern cottage (too many are being torn down these days, when fashion favors beachside behemoths and mountain mastodons), or of building a new one that reflects the spirit of old-time southern cottages.

Antique wicker charmingly furnishes the commodious porch of Shadowland, *an Arts and Crafts cottage in Troutville, Virginia.*

southern

shores

spirit
house

AN EARLY-TWENTIETH-CENTURY BEACH SHACK

Folly Beach, South Carolina ᨏᨏ

The word "cottage" has broad applications, referring equally to large, rambling houses sheathed with shingles and tiny one-room structures with walls so thin that the sunlight peeks between the boards. There are urban cottages, such as New Orleans' Creole cottages, and rural ones, like fish camps, mountain escapes, and seaside retreats, but what they all have in common is an abundance of simple charm and a minimum of architectural frills.

One of the most basic types of cottage is the one-room beach shack—little more than a glorified cabana that provides a place to sleep and get out of the sun, a porch to catch the breeze, and pared-down cooking and bathing facilities. This is the kind of cottage interior designer Amelia Handegan chose for her own private getaway on Folly Beach, an island near Charleston, South Carolina, where her bustling firm and showroom is located.

"I've always been looking for a little shack over there," explains the South Carolina native, who also owns an early-nineteenth-century plantation-style house in downtown Charleston. Although her design projects tend toward the grand, she craved something small and simple as a place to retreat and recharge. As the mother of two teenage sons, Amelia "wanted someplace to go

The beach-side façade is covered by a screened porch that nearly doubles the tiny
cottage's size. Sky-blue posts add a touch of color. Surrounded by trees and caressed
by ocean breezes, the cottage is surprisingly cool in the summer months.

Above: *The size of a dollhouse, this antique spirit house from Indonesia is said to invite benevolent spirits to spread their protective grace over the home where the sculpture is placed.*

Opposite: *Amelia loves Indian textiles and has collected these colorful examples over the years. A German educational diagram illustrating jellyfish adds an appropriately marine element of whimsy to the porch's décor.*

that was mine, that was away from it all, and that nurtured my inner spirit."

One morning after a walk on Folly Beach, Amelia saw a real estate agent placing flyers in a tube next to a grassy driveway and stopped to inquire about the property. The next day, she made an offer. The little one-room structure, placed in the center of a lot with a view of the marsh on one side and just a block away from the ocean on the other, was exactly what she was seeking. "Even though the lot is small, it gives the impression of being utterly secluded because it has so many trees growing on it," says Amelia—five old oak trees, and twenty-five others including hollies and magnolias, to be exact.

The sound of the wind is constant here, with a murmur of rustling vegetation that keeps Amelia from feeling too alone. The cottage provides a cozy nook perfect for the solitary pleasures of reading, painting, and resting—particularly now that Amelia has reshaped it, adding a sleeping alcove that contributes another sixty-four square feet to the structure's original two-hundred-square-foot room. Including the porch and a tiny bathroom, the entire house has less than five hundred square feet, and that suits Amelia fine: "Every day I am involved in large houses, so it is nice to have such a little place where I can relax."

After she bought the house four years ago, Amelia had to work to transform the homely space into one that would feed and express her passion for sensual surroundings. First, she designed the new alcove, with windows on three sides and a curtained wall where she can drift to sleep lulled by island breezes. Then she turned her attention to the large room, opening up the

ceiling to expose rafters and crossbeams, using the added height to visually enlarge the space. She painted the ceilings, walls, and floor white, increasing the illusion of space, and designed bookshelves on one end and a simple kitchen on the other. Two countertop-height refrigerators and a tiny dishwasher make the kitchen appliances almost unnoticeable. Open shelving provides ample storage for a basic array of tableware and cookware.

Amelia also rehabilitated the little bathroom, originally a concrete add-on devoid of charm. She covered the walls with white tile, topped with a decorative frieze of seashells that supports a narrow ledge for toiletries. A white curtain suspended by strings of tiny shells encloses the corner shower. Amelia also hired a local craftsman to build an outdoor shower from bamboo beneath the shade of an oak tree. This is Amelia's favorite place to rinse off after a run on the beach or a bike ride.

A deck was added on a spot of land overlooking the marsh, providing for an ideal place to entertain friends. Originally Amelia had a beautiful tent from India covering it, but a storm blew it down. Now the deck is simply furnished with bamboo chairs and a bronze basin perfect for fires in the winter or floating flowers in the summer months. A carved wood spirit house from Indonesia perches on a long seat that parallels the marsh's edge. Intricately crafted, the wooden sculpture is a miniature replica of a traditional

Vintage bamboo chairs offers comfortable seating in the living room, while a table tucked into a nook can serve as dining table, worktable, or pure decoration when covered with an antique Indian textile embroidered with mirror sequins.

Indonesian home, with steeply slanting gables, decorated cornices, and curvilinear balustrades. Spirit houses are traditionally placed outside the entrances of Indonesian homes to invite good spirits. Amelia hopes that this one may help to ward off destructive visitations in the form of hurricanes, which pose a danger to vulnerable barrier islands like Folly Beach. When she decorated her island escape, she tried to use items that were not irreplaceable. "I thought I'd fill it with things that weren't all that valuable so if they washed out to sea, I wouldn't care," she explains, adding "but I would care."

With the exception of the porch, which is decorated with brightly colored Indian textiles and sky-blue architectural details, the house's color scheme is white-on-white. White flokati carpets cover the woven sisal rug on the main room's floor. Amelia put the rugs down in the wintertime when the cottage felt chilly, but found that she loved their soft, fluffy texture in the summer as well. An Indian textile of white fabric embroidered with mirror sequins covers a table tucked between the bookcases at one end of the room. White slipcovers drape a pair of folding chairs placed on either side of a chest. Vintage bamboo chairs provide additional seating, decorated with throw pillows studded with large mirror sequins.

Natural brown tones add contrast to the pale palette: the honey color of the bamboo furniture, the dark brown finish of a late-nineteenth-century American chest of drawers, the golden transparency of a giant elephant ear leaf dried and mounted on a white mat. The last is one of two pressed botanical specimens that serve as artwork on the cottage's walls. Darkened metal objects add further visual interest to

the space, including an exotic bronze hanging lamp in the main room and two Moroccan sconces of pierced metal in the alcove.

Despite its diminutive size, elemental nature, and spare palette, the cottage's interior is still unmistakably the creation of Amelia Handegan. This designer's deft ability to marry the exotic with the familiar, the primitive with the refined, and elements from nature with fine objects made by hand is distinctly her own.

Above left: *Faint tracery of decorative painting can still be discerned on a late-nineteenth-century American chest of drawers that Amelia found during her flea market forays. A pressed and framed botanical element in the living room echoes the cottage's surrounding landscape of lush tropical plants.*

Left: *A sculptural object combining a turned-wood candlestick with a starfish and sea fan captured Amelia's attention at an antiques mall. She found the alabaster bedside lamp at a flea market and paired it with a parchment shade.*

Opposite: *A white-on-white palette of textiles, including flokati carpets, canvas cushions, embroidered curtains, and an appliqué Indian bedspread create a mood at once serene and sensual within the bedroom.*

endless summer

AN EARLY-TWENTIETH-CENTURY COTTAGE
WITH A NEW ADDITION

Atlantic Beach, Florida

Florida is the land of endless summer, with bright waters surrounding more than two-thirds of its border and a climate that rarely dips below freezing. Northeasterners and midwesterners have long traveled there to partake of its gentle winters, while the natives are loath to leave its balmy shores. Mac Easton, an avid surfer who grew up in Miami and Key Biscayne, is such a Floridian. "I've always known I wanted to live somewhere where there was surf," he says. His wife Jill, from Tarpon Springs, Florida, is just as fervent about being near the sea.

The two began their life together along the beaches outside Jacksonville, where Mac's grandparents lived. There's something for every beach lover there, from the high-end community of Ponte Vedra to the more casual charms of Jacksonville Beach and Atlantic Beach, which is where the couple eventually found their beachfront cottage. The towns' architecture varies, ranging from large Shingle-style homes to small Cape Cod houses and tiny bungalows, mostly dating from the late nineteenth century to the first decades of the twentieth. What unites these houses, however, is simplicity of design and sympathy with the landscape—a long stretch of grassy dunes paralleling a white beach on

The new house presents a traditional Shingle-style façade,
with its hipped roof and gable supported by brackets and
a porch poised above white-painted pillars.

one side and a low canopy of scrub trees on the other. The vernacular architecture was originally built of resilient local cypress, with cypress shingles covering the exteriors and walls of cypress paneling within. Pine, also plentiful in Florida, was often combined with the cypress, and later cedar shakes and shingles were added to the mix. These houses, which reflect a blend of northeastern and southern influences, nestle into dips and perch on the peaks of dunes and bluffs, looking out across the ultramarine sea. It was this charming manmade environment, in addition to the ever-ready surf, that appealed to the Eastons.

The small cottage they eventually chose was built in the 1930s and inhabited for several decades by a retired admiral. With a living room and two bedrooms as narrow as ships' galleys upstairs, and another bedroom and a kitchen/dining area below, it was just big enough for the Eastons and their young children, Abbe and C. J. "We definitely lived the simple life," says Jill, who painted the dark pine tongue-and-groove interior paneling white in an effort to brighten up the rooms and make them seem larger. But no amount of illusion was going to make the house large enough when baby number three was on the way. "We knew we needed a bigger house, but I didn't want to tear the cottage down," says Jill.

Instead, the couple decided to build a second house in front of the cottage on the large plot of land

A pool patio of limestone, sheltered between the two structures, provides a retreat from the hot sun and breezy beach. Blue stucco details reflect the hue of cooling waters and contrast with the warm brown shingle siding.

that stretched to the dunes. They hired Karen Rutter of Jacksonville to design a spacious house with a modern, open plan of rooms within a traditional Shingle-style exterior. "Mac and Jill liked the cedar shake cottages of the area, but their taste is for more modern design," says Karen. "My challenge was to integrate these two styles." Employing warm brown shingles accented with white trim to unite the two structures visually, the architect physically joined them with a second-story bridge. A sign pronouncing "Endless Summer" hangs from this open-air walkway, where grown-ups, children, dogs, and cats promenade throughout the year.

The interior of the new house has a distinctly contemporary appearance, with the second story's open floor plan, soaring ceilings, and walls of windows. This modern mood is tempered by an abundance of heart pine details that reconnect the interior with the local building traditions. This element came into the mix when Mac purchased an old warehouse in the Jacksonville area and began salvaging the old heart pine from which it was made; he appreciates the wood's soft, burnt-red appearance. The couple then hired interior designer Kathleen Hines to integrate this collection of beams, floorboards, and paneling into the design. "Heart pine can create a rustic, country feel, but I wanted to use this material in a way that was fresher, more modern," says Kathleen. She recommended covering the floors with dark honey-colored pine polished to a glossy sheen. Heart pine pillars measuring fifteen-by-seventeen inches form exposed structural supports, and three-by-eleven-inch beams span the ceilings in the dining and living room areas.

Above: *A covered walkway connects the old guest cottage to the new house, allowing visitors to enter the kitchen and breakfast room area, which leads into the oceanfront dining and living rooms. The exposed pulley of a dumbwaiter that travels from the kitchen to the ground floor level adds visual interest.*

Opposite: *Contemporary lighting, furniture, and art (including a pastel drawing of a fiddlehead fern by John Buck) create uncluttered elegance in the dining room.*

Overleaf: *A rough-hewn oak railway pallet creates a sculptural coffee table in the living room, where paintings of palm trees by Robert Flynn echo the view from the windows.*

A shorter beam, attached horizontally to the living room wall above the fireplace, makes a mantel-like ledge perfect for holding flowers and candles. A fireplace surround of blue glass mosaic tile offers cool, contemporary contrast.

The couple hired a friend and interior designer, Allison Hillis, as a third member of the design team. She helped them select the boxy armchairs and sofa slipcovered in white, along with an antique Persian carpet, which form a casually elegant seating area around the fireplace. In another seating space, she chose a pair of turn-of-the-century French chairs reminiscent of ocean-liner deck chairs that turn to face the sea. A replica of a 1930s paddle surfboard designed by legendary surfer Tom Blake hangs above the chairs, a reminder of Mac's favorite pastime; more like a kayak than a surfboard, the hollow board looks as gracefully unwieldy as one of the Wright brothers' airplanes.

The new house follows a traditional seaside plan, with bedrooms arranged on the lower floor and the entertaining areas poised above it to capture views and breezes from the sea. The lower floor includes three bedrooms for the children and a master suite for the parents. "Every day I wake up and watch the ocean," says Mac, who sleeps in a master bedroom with windows that frame the sea. A long central hallway of toe-cooling tile runs through the space, connecting the limestone-paved courtyard between the original cottage and the new house with a grassy lawn that slopes down toward the beach.

In contrast to the bedroom floor, which has a restful, well-shaded atmosphere perfect for sleep and

retreat from the Florida heat, the second floor is bright and open, with walls of glass that frame constantly changing vistas of the sea and sky. While these apertures have a distinctly modern appearance from the inside, forming a rhythmic geometry of light, when viewed from without they present a more traditional configuration of French doors topped by transoms and surrounded by sidelights. "We always wanted to live by the sea," says Jill, "but I never imagined a house like this, where I can see the sea from nearly every room, and feel it everywhere around me."

Today, the small original cottage functions as a guesthouse, accommodating a constant flow of visiting family and friends. With a sheltered pool courtyard, the easy-flowing gathering spaces of the main floor, and a long porch and large lawn open to the sea and sky, the house invites all who gather there to partake freely of the adventure of Florida's endless summer.

Opposite: *A wall with an interior window separates the kitchen from casual family gathering spaces, including a billiard room and den. The central seating area has a soaring two-story ceiling illuminated by clerestory windows. On either side of it, lower ceilings accented with exposed beams of heart pine create a more intimate feeling in the living and dining rooms.*

Above: *White-painted, cottage-style furniture decorates daughter Abbe's room, where kiwi-green walls offer bright contrast to the house's predominate palette of woodtones and white.*

work of sensitive developers and their architects who created guidelines directing every aspect of design for the two adjacent developments, from scale and proportion to details and materials.

Taking cues from the vernacular architecture of the American South and the Caribbean, the houses of WaterColor are inviting structures with porches that are easy to sit on, windows that open wide, and rooms that breathe. Jim Strickland, founder of Historical Concepts, an architecture and land planning company based in Atlanta, was one of the team leaders who developed the guidelines and prototypes. When he and his wife Linda decided to build their own second home there, Jim brought to the task both his professional training as a Yale-educated architect and his personal experience as a southerner who had long summered at similar beaches.

Although the Stricklands' cottage is less than ten years old, it is already what Jim calls "a generational building," providing a friendly environment for three generations of his extended family and looking as though it has been doing so for a century. In part, Jim created this illusion by drawing upon a cottage form employed widely in the South in the 1920s and 1930s known as a hip-roof bungalow. A sloping roof of tin reflects the sun's rays and deflects storm winds, while providing ceiling height within to draw heat up and out through dormer windows projecting from all four sides. A shaded porch accommodates a cool indoor-outdoor space at the front of the house and invites breezes to flow within.

While the architect borrowed ideas from houses in the Caribbean and Cuban cigar makers' houses in the Florida Keys for the porch, including the lower walls

of wood slats with decorative cutouts and the tall louvered shutters, the interior is pure South. Old wicker, painted wood tables, and a huge mahogany wardrobe furnish the large living, dining, and kitchen area that spans the front half of the house. Fishing rods, bright red oars, tackle boxes, and leaping fish mounted on walls and ceiling beams suggest the simple pleasures of a fish camp. Vintage gas and kerosene lanterns rewired for electricity hang from the ceiling. Collections of shells and coral fill bowls and cover surfaces.

Jim went on a year-long shopping spree to furnish and decorate the house, visiting his favorite antiques shops and purveyors of specialty products, including vintage lighting expert Eloise Pickard and reclaimed heart pine dealer Willis Everett. A stuffed bison head, dubbed "Willis the Water Buffalo" by the Strickland family, also came from Everett, after his wife suggested he find a new home for it. Once Hilton Head–based interior designer Ruth Edwards decided that Jim had found enough southern vernacular accessories, she pulled together his purchases with colorful quilts and white slipcovers, framed maps and family photos to create a home that feels subtly sophisticated, effortlessly old-fashioned, and immeasurably comfortable.

"Our mantra was for this to be a place where the grandkids could jump up and down and spill ice cream, the dogs could jump up and down and

The conch houses of Key West often feature porches like this, with slats pierced with decorative details topped by tall, louvered shutters that invite light and air while protecting the interior from excessive sun and wind. Jim borrowed the idea of the canvas curtain for the porch entrance from a house he saw in Brunswick, Georgia.

shed," explains Jim. Linda, who shares the house with her sister Karen Vance's family, agrees: "It's a place meant for family, not for show. I wanted it to be comfortable and easy to maintain. You can open all the French doors and let the wind blow everything around and it doesn't matter." Jim says that this is reminiscent of the atmosphere when they were children, pointing to the triple row of family photographs hanging in the stair hall that date from the early twentieth century to the present, depicting several generations of the family relaxing on southern shores.

The grandchildren have the run of the house, often resting tired limbs on oversized chairs and sofas in the living area, drawing or playing games on the long dining room table, or telling stories and taking naps on the front porch, where shutters and canvas curtains can be closed to create a private and sheltered outdoor space. Their exclusive domain is the entire second floor, where a large room houses a pair of beds tucked into twin alcoves beneath opposing eaves of the hipped roof. Drawing their curtains shut, each child can claim his bed as a private place, including a play area nestled between bed and window.

While the house looks like a small bungalow from the front, efficient use of space actually accommodates three more bedrooms on the ground floor: two small

In the living area, floors of two-hundred-year-old heart pine that has been whitewashed, sanded, buffed, and waxed lend an appearance of age. Whitewashed boards of new pine clad the walls, creating a luminous backdrop for turquoise window surrounds, painted furniture, and rustic artifacts including fishing rods and oars.

ones on one side of the stair hall and a larger master bedroom suite on the other. Each bedroom has its own full bath (including a luxuriously large clawfooted tub in the master bath), and there is a powder room as well. Other conveniences include built-in drawers in each room and closets hung with curtains instead of doors that are just the right size for a week's worth of summer clothes.

The house can sleep twelve people or more, and a dozen can sit comfortably at the long table that Jim designed from leftover heart pine flooring. He tried to finish the table himself, but admits to putting on the wrong paint and then trying unsuccessfully to remove it, creating a slightly mottled appearance. "Now we have all the marks left by the children's art projects, too, so we've ended up with our own patina," he says, quite contentedly.

Patina, combined with vernacular style and traditional materials, is the magic ingredient that creates the cottage's perfect atmosphere of old-time southern charm. Although it resides on the surface of an object, patina reflects its soul, speaking of the passage of time, the touch of hands, the effects of the elements. Patina transforms an object that is shiny and new into something that has been knocked around a bit and seen a thing or two. An object that has patina looks like it has a good story to tell, and so does the Stricklands' cottage—even if it is a bit of a tall fish tale.

Opposite: *Light flows down into the first floor through a wide transom window over the entrance to the stair hall, which is lined with old photographs showing generations of the family summering at southern beaches.*

Above: *Striped curtains lend a playful mood to the living room where leisure is the theme, expressed through baskets filled with paperbacks, games including an antique French lawn bowling set, and shells collected during beachside expeditions.*

Overleaf: *A rustic table made from planks of two-hundred-year-old heart pine can be pulled away from the kitchen island to seat twelve for large gatherings, or used as shown for smaller meals and children's art projects.*

Below: *A partition wall separating the bathing area from the toilet in the master bathroom stops shy of the ceiling, allowing for the flow of light and air through louvered shutters of transom windows placed high in the exterior walls.*

Opposite: *The guest bedroom is just large enough for a double bed and bureau. More storage space is created by built-in drawers and a closet concealed behind a curtain that coordinates with the bed's old-fashioned floral spread.*

Above: *Two old tin vanities were refinished and replumbed to create a Jack-and-Jill bathroom for the grandchildren.*

unpainted aristocracy

A TRADITIONAL BEACH COTTAGE, CIRCA 1900

Nags Head, North Carolina ～

Yes, I guess I am guilty of the 'unpainted aristocracy' line," wrote Jonathan Daniels, editor of Raleigh's *News and Observer*, in a letter from 1976. "Those were charming old beach houses even if you could sometimes look through the floor and see the sand fiddlers." Daniels was addressing Catherine Bishir, author of an article for the *North Carolina Historical Review*, later published as a booklet titled *The "Unpainted Aristocracy": The Beach Cottages of Old Nags Head*. His term "unpainted aristocracy" refers to a mile-long row of dark brown shingled houses that have stood upon pilings on the sands of Nags Head since the late nineteenth and early twentieth centuries.

The summer home of John and Caroline Trask of Beaufort, South Carolina, is among these historic dwellings. Their family has owned the cottage since the 1930s, when Caroline's grandfather and uncle acquired it through a business deal. It was built in the late nineteenth or early twentieth century as a simple fisherman's dwelling on the Roanoke Sound side of the island, but was subsequently moved to the ocean side, where it remains with the other members of the "unpainted aristocracy."

The diagonal lines of gabled roofs, dormers, and batten awning shutters propped aloft are common features of the late-nineteenth- and early-twentieth-century houses that comprise Nags Head's Unpainted Aristocracy.

Like the dunes that shift constantly in the currents of wind and water that caress, and sometimes careen wildly over, North Carolina's Outer Banks, these houses have survived through a combination of mobility and adaptability. While it is hard to imagine these hulking structures moving and changing with ease, they have done just that, again and again. Like the Trask house, many originated as smaller cottages facing the Roanoke Sound separating Nags Head from the North Carolina mainland. They were built, for the most part, by well-to-do North Carolinians and Virginians as simple summer getaways.

Mainlanders began summering on Nags Head as early as 1830. Some built unpretentious homes, and others stayed at grand seaside hotels boasting ballrooms, horse-drawn railroads, and boardwalks traversing the island from sound to sea. After the Civil War, it became fashionable to own cottages on the ocean side of the island. Some homeowners had their cottages placed on rollers and moved across the narrow island. Others built new ones in a practical vernacular style that came to be associated with Nags Head. "The dictates of survival and convenience on the weather-battered Outer Banks, not the whims of fashion, dictated the form and detail," wrote Bishir. Her description continues:

The cottages stand high on their timber pilings, well above the low waves that lap along the beach. Between the pilings is often stretched a

A piece of driftwood in the shape of a goose was collected from the beach by Caroline Trask's grandmother. The simply furnished dining room has changed little since she decorated it decades ago.

latticework screen—originally to keep out the wandering pig and cow population. . . . The walls . . . are covered with unpainted siding or wooden shingles, weathered to a rich gray-brown in the salt air. Protection from sun in summer and from storms in other seasons is provided by wood batten shutters, hinged at the top and, to capture the languid winds, held open with a prop stick. . . . Expanding the interiors of the cottages are the broad porches, skirting two, three, and even four sides of the houses. Ubiquitous benches emerge from simple wooden porch railings and slant out over the thin air to catch the ocean breezes. To the rear of the cottages . . . are separate kitchens, linked by breezeways and often separate wings for the servants.

These words perfectly describe the Trasks' cottage, where Caroline has spent every summer of her life since 1939. The house was a two-story, L-shaped structure back then, with a kitchen, dining room, living room, and bedroom on the first floor and two more bedrooms above. Its shape was designed to make the most of the ocean breezes, with windows placed on at least two sides of each room. When the house was enlarged in the 1950s, the L-shape was simply elongated, creating room above for two more bedrooms, and for a large kitchen and expanded living room below. All of the rooms open directly onto porches that accommodate wide benches along the perimeter, making for expansive outdoor living spaces.

Caroline still spends a full summer at the house each year, sharing it with her husband and visiting sisters, children, and grandchildren. Although Nags Head has changed a lot, with endless strip malls and motels,

she faithfully maintains the simple lifestyle she remembers enjoying as a child: "We get up in the morning and go for walks on the beach. We do a lot of reading. I will not allow a television set in the cottage. And we have no air-conditioning."

The family usually eats lunch on the porch, sitting in commodious Adirondack-style chairs, wooden rockers, or benches, and enjoying meals set out upon trays. In the evenings, they gather in the dining room, which is furnished exactly as Caroline remembers it from meals presided over by her grandmother, Louise Wilson Clark, and grandfather, Sam Nash Clark. A selection of mismatched ladder-back chairs line the narrow room, and a large sideboard filled with china dominates one wall. Caroline's grandmother bought the sideboard in the nearby town of Currituck for just a few dollars. The table is often set with her grandmother's china, although recently Caroline purchased a new set of pale-turquoise-glazed dishware.

Nearly all of the furniture and decorative objects in the house are the same as they have been for three-quarters of a century. Bamboo furniture offers comfortable seating in the living room. Iron bedsteads and simple wood furniture painted white fill the bedrooms. Old grass rugs cover the painted wood floors. Pieces of driftwood and large shells collected by Caroline's grandmother, an enthusiastic beachcomber, adorn the walls and sit upon mantels, in baskets, and on

Bamboo furniture from the 1930s has provided comfortable seating in the living room for generations. The mounted fish on the wall was caught by Caroline's son while fishing with his grandfather. The spectacular catch was celebrated in the local newspaper with the headline "Little Boy Catches Big Fish."

Unpainted Aristocracy 53

tabletops. Among her treasures are the spinal disks of a whale found by a friend at nearby Whalebone Junction. These grace the mantel in the living room—a mantel without a working fireplace, or even a chimney standing behind it. The chimney was lost in 1998, when a bad nor'easter whipped the island with high winds and tides and nearly destroyed the house.

"After that, the house was *in* the ocean," recalls Caroline. Fortunately, she and her husband owned the lot to the north, to which they moved the house. It was the third time the house had been moved in Caroline's lifetime. And yet despite the relentless energy of the ocean, the lazy rhythms of life inside the house continue unchanged. "The days go by so fast," says Caroline. "You bring projects that you think you're going to work on, and you never do. We take a two-hour nap every day. We visit each other and see family."

Nags Head, as viewed from the porches of the houses that comprise the "unpainted aristocracy," seems unchanged as well. Lying in a hammock, with views of the dunes' tenacious grasses and wildflowers, white sands, and the watery horizon bracketed only by the dark-shingled walls of similar houses, it's easy to drift in timeless reverie. "The sense of continuity and love of families for Nags Head have prevailed against fierce storms and development alike," writes Bishir. "The mile-long row of cottages, weathered dark and rich with summer memories, survives."

Opposite: *An antique drop-leaf table, which was in the kitchen before Caroline moved it to its new place beneath the stairs, holds a precious stack of guest books that date back to 1937. "Everybody who has stayed here since has signed it," says Caroline. "We're on our fourth book."*

Above: *This bedroom, added during the mid-1950s expansion of the house, is still called Uncle Russell's room, even though he departed this life thirty years ago. Its plain, painted furniture remains unchanged since his occupancy.*

Above: *Brown shingles, crisscrossing lattice, and a rope hammock form a familiar porch scene shared by cottages to the right and the left of the Trask family home.*

Right: *Wide, breezy porches sheltered by shed roofs expand the living space of the old cottages of Nags Head, creating comfortable outdoor sitting, dining, and even sleeping space.*

tybee
time

A RAISED COTTAGE, CIRCA 1900

Tybee Island, Georgia ⌁

Being on Tybee Time, that's what we call it," says Erica Wilson, explaining why she and her husband, Tad, bought a cottage getaway less than a half-hour away from their primary residence on another island near Savannah, Georgia. "Tybee is all about flip-flops and being very, very casual. Everybody knows everybody. When my husband drives out here," she says of Tad, an orthopedic surgeon, "he feels like he is really getting away."

When the couple bought the neglected house two years ago, the renovation it required might have seemed like a major headache to some prospective owners. "When Tad said he wanted to make an offer, I thought he was crazy," recalls Erica, who was expecting their third child at the time. But the couple had been longing for a house on the water that could accommodate their growing family. When they saw the hipped-roof house with wraparound porches commanding a point where the Back River flows out into the Atlantic Ocean, Tad knew at once it was the cottage of his dreams.

After touring the interior, which was the victim of general decay and a regrettable 1970s renovation involving hung acoustical tile ceilings, luan paneling, and sliding glass doors, the couple decided to get a second opinion from their friend, Jane Coslick, a preservationist who has been

Elevated on pilings and stretching wide to catch cool sea breezes beneath its low hipped roof, the Wilsons' cottage is built in a vernacular style that was popular on Tybee Island in the late nineteenth and early twentieth centuries.

Above: *The long porch facing the ocean has several different areas, including this serene sitting area outside the master bedroom.*

Right: *The Wilsons extended the porch by sixteen feet, replacing a narrow deck with a wide screened porch complete with a handmade pine railing that provides a period feel. Antique wicker furniture that came with the house also lends timeless appeal.*

renovating old houses and cottages in the area for twenty-five years. "Jane gave us the thumbs up, so we bought the house," Erica recounts. They also hired her as their designer and project manager for the complex restoration.

Jane spent more than a year solving the day-to-day issues of renovation and identifying compatible construction methods and materials. Her goal was to maintain the integrity of the cottage while meeting the family's needs and desires. The kitchen, master bedroom, and master bath designs called for a creative mix of materials in order to produce a viable blending of the old and the new.

Viewed from the raised walkway that leads to the house over the beach dunes, the cottage looks quite large. It was built around 1900 by Captain Saucey, who constructed a row of nearly identical houses along this stretch of land for Savannah summerers. In what became a popular vernacular Tybee form, these houses of Captain's Row are long and narrow, raised above potential storm surges on pilings, and capped with low hipped roofs of tin that deflect the sun. Sheltered porches that run around the sides provide outdoor spaces for living and sleeping while diffusing light and capturing breezes that cool interior rooms.

The families who owned the cottage previously introduced changes over the years, converting a small

wing that may have once been a kitchen house into guest quarters, adding a dank kitchen on the ground floor level, and constructing an ugly carport. The Wilsons renovated the guest wing into an airy suite of rooms, moved the kitchen back to the main living floor, and tore down the carport. When they moved the kitchen, they lost the master bedroom, so the couple decided to turn the sleeping porch on the side of the house into a new and spacious bedroom suite with expansive ocean views.

Once these decisions were made, it was easy to re-envision the house's large central space as an open, light-filled area where kitchen, dining, and living rooms could seamlessly blend. Part of the old wall separating the original master bedroom and the living area was removed, opening the kitchen to the rest of the space. Jane suggested creating a dining bay by bumping out one end of the new kitchen into the porch. With windows in two walls and French doors opening onto the porch, the room feels almost like an outdoor dining room.

Jane brought in carpenter Bruce McNall, who had thirty years of experience in the area, to assist with the project. He recommended taking the interior down to the studs, stripping all the old heart pine paneling and returning it, with a fresh coat of paint, to its original place. The result is a series of interior rooms that feel as though they have always been just as they are. These include a bunk room at the far end of the living room where the Wilsons' son and daughter sleep, and the tiny nursery off the master bedroom for baby Grace. Born a few months after the house was purchased, the house shares her name—Amazing Grace.

Opposite: A great deal of work went into creating the effortless charm of the living room. The original heart pine floors and pine-paneled walls were taken out, stripped, and then returned to their places. A new fireplace was built to provide a focal point at the end of the room. Window openings were extended down to the floor and transoms added above doorways to allow for more natural light and air circulation.

Above: *Surrounded on three sides by windows and French doors, the dining alcove was created by building a bay that extends out from the kitchen. Erica Wilson found the oyster shell chandelier by local artisan James Adams at Savannah's Paris Flea Market.*

Opposite: *Glass mosaic tile adorns the kitchen counter and living room fireplace. Erica, who makes biannual antiquing expeditions to North Carolina, found the bronze mermaid that lounges above the kitchen counter during one such trip.*

While the renovations took careful planning and time, today the Wilsons love their waterfront cottage. "Many people would have just mowed this house down," says Erica. "People thought we were crazy. Even my husband asked, at one point, 'What are we getting ourselves into?'" The family comes to the house every weekend in the winter and lives here all summer, making the most of their surroundings. "My children are addicted to playing in the sand and discovering the animals that live in the ocean—the horseshoe crabs and blue crabs, and the turtle nests," says Erica. Amazing Grace has turned out to be a much needed playground for the adult Wilsons as well, who go biking or take a john boat (a flat-bottomed motor boat) out into the river and explore all the waterways.

The cottage also provides the perfect place to gather with their friends, and according to Erica, everyone usually ends up relaxing out on the porch. Even when they are alone, the porch is the place to be, she says: "We live on the porch—in the morning it's so nice there. We love to watch the birds. The other day, we spotted a great horned owl up in one of our trees. We can't imagine being anywhere else in the summer."

Opposite: *Erica found many of the bathroom's vintage accoutrements during what she calls her "junking expeditions" to North Carolina.*

Above: *This airy master bedroom suite was created by enclosing a sleeping porch. The walls are covered with new butt-jointed spruce that complements the old pine paneling used throughout the rest of the house.*

abiding style

A MODERN SHINGLE-STYLE COTTAGE

Atlantic Beach, Florida ∼

T he Petway family has always loved Atlantic Beach, an old-fashioned beach community outside of Jacksonville. Florida native Tom Petway has been visiting here since childhood. When he and his wife Betty decided to relocate their primary residence from Jacksonville to Atlantic Beach, they knew they wanted a place that captured the traditional charm for which the community's late-nineteenth- and early-twentieth-century cottages are beloved. However, they also wanted a new house built to meet their needs, including plentiful rooms for entertaining family and friends, porches for enjoying the views, and guest rooms to house visitors.

The couple didn't have to look far for an architect, selecting Jacksonville native Richard Skinner, who had designed their previous residence and excelled in building new houses in traditional styles, whether formal neoclassical mansions or relaxed seaside homes that creatively interpret the Shingle style. Richard grew up going to Atlantic Beach and was very familiar with its beach houses, so the couple was confident that he could design a comfortable beach cottage that would fit in with the environment and look like it had been there for years. They also trusted him to overcome the challenge of building on the long, narrow slice of beachside bluff they had chosen for their house site.

The Petway family's new cottage, designed by Jacksonville architect Richard Skinner,
takes advantage of the irregular massing of Shingle-style architecture to create a varied
and engaging edifice that perches upon a bluff without dominating the landscape.

Rising on a high bluff covered with sea oats, the four-bedroom house appears deceptively small when viewed from the beach below. The architect created this illusion by breaking up the beach-side façade into a series of receding planes with irregularly spaced windows, varied rooflines, and asymmetrical porches. "The beauty of this style is that it allows you to break the scale down, so you don't end up with those grand houses by the beach that look as if they belong in the suburbs," explains Richard.

Asymmetry is one of the typical aspects of the Shingle style, which developed in New England's coastal regions in the late nineteenth century. It grew out of the Queen Anne houses of the late Victorian era and became the style of choice for the beach cottages of New England's rich and famous. When many of these northerners began coming by rail to winter along Florida's coast, they brought the style with them. This helps explain why these dark-shingled, white-trimmed, rambling cottages closely associated with the Northeast are so prevalent along this southern beach.

Because the Petways' house is elevated upon a bluff, it affords views not only of the ocean, but also the surrounding landscape. While the house's living room, kitchen, and family room all feature ocean views, there are also spaces designed to make the most of the softer light and cool shelter of the house's western exposure. Richard drew one element of the design from an old cottage he recalled that had a room at the back of the house where everyone gathered to enjoy breakfast. "Because it was sheltered, they didn't have the bright sun in their eyes," he explains. With this idea in mind, he designed a shady nook of a den on the land side of the house, as well as a porch facing westward, which provides Betty a place to enjoy the sunset and the westerly views.

However, the main focus of the house is the ocean and the wide sky above, viewed from banks of easterly windows, two beach-side porches, and a wide deck. This elemental view inspired the blue-and-white color scheme chosen by Atlanta-based interior designer Jackye Lanham, who decorated the Petways' previous beach cottage and was their seaside neighbor. As a southerner, she combines an appreciation of the region's relaxed charm with an understanding of the sophisticated mix of English and tropical elements that informs its decorative arts. Like Richard, she excels in marrying traditional design with a contemporary sensibility.

The Petways already had a collection of European, British, and Irish antiques that Jackye used to anchor the designs for each room. They bring an English country feel to the living and dining rooms on the first floor, complementing the rustic exposed beams that traverse the ceiling. This long room is visually divided into discrete spaces for gathering and dining by articulated ceiling elements and a folding screen of wood and glass. Jackye balances the dark tones of the room's wooden pieces with sheer white curtains veiling a wall of windows, blue-and-white striped rugs she custom designed, and pale beige bouclé upholstery on the sofas.

Another long room parallels the living room—a more casual family gathering place that includes a kitchen with a large central island, a dining area, and

Atlanta-based designer Jackye Lanham combines English, Irish, and European antiques with contemporary upholstered pieces and carpets to create a mood that is at once elegant and relaxed in the living room.

Left: *Shingle-style houses typically feature windows in a variety of shapes and sizes, including the oval form shown here in the dining room. With its long wall of books and single window, the room has an intimate, enclosed feeling even though it actually opens onto the living room.*

Above: *In keeping with the English Arts and Crafts tradition that influenced America's Shingle-style architecture, Betty Petway sets her dining table with hand-thrown and glazed pottery.*

Above: *A Biedermeier table of applewood is one of Betty's favorite antiques. She often seats casual dinner gatherings around this table, which overlooks the kitchen on one end and a bank of windows facing the ocean on the other.*

Opposite: *The family sitting room next to the kitchen still retains the feeling of the wraparound porch it was once intended to be during the design process. With plentiful windows and curtains, the Petways can have as much or as little exposure to the elements as they wish in this inviting space.*

a sitting area surrounded by wraparound windows. Richard originally envisioned this last area as a porch, but the Petways preferred it as an indoor, air-conditioned space; the result is a room that seems simply to melt away into the surrounding space, whether the long, sheer white curtains are drawn open to reveal the ocean view, or pulled shut to reflect the sky's radiance.

A pair of chairs with backs of woven natural fiber flanks a stucco and stone fireplace, adding rustic texture to the family room, also decorated in a palette of blue and white. Bamboo chairs encircle a Biedermeier table that is one of Betty's favorite antiques. This table, which can be extended with leaves, is both a favorite breakfast spot and casual dining area for larger gatherings. With dining possibilities ranging from the formal dining room to informal arrangements in the kitchen or on the porches, the house beautifully accommodates the Petways' love of entertaining friends and their extended family.

Although both of the Petways' adult children have homes in Atlantic Beach, the couple still enjoys occasional overnight visits from their grandchildren, as well as visiting friends. The second floor is designed to easily sleep several guests, with two guest bedrooms, each with private baths, opening off the stair hall. Dark-stained contemporary furniture and bold tropical prints lend verve to the first guest room, recalling the dark mahogany and hand-dyed textiles of the Caribbean islands. The second, which overlooks the sea, echoes the view with a palette of white painted wood and wicker furniture mixed with white and blue textiles for airy charm. A guesthouse positioned behind the main house offers further room for visitors.

The master bedroom is a spacious chamber, with large windows framing views of the ocean. Curtains and Roman shades of opaque blue and beige fabric temper the light that pours in at dawn. The walls and ceilings are covered with tongue-and-groove paneling, a material that the architect likes to use in keeping with local building traditions. "In many of the old cottages I've seen here, rooms have cypress tongue-and-groove siding," says Richard. "I use as much of this paneling as I can because it is simple and straight-forward. It gives the eye a place to relax and imparts a sense of longevity."

The paneling in the Petways' bedroom, painted white on the walls and pale blue on the ceiling, also fulfills this intention, evoking memories of restful southern porches. A porch swing on a balcony outside the bedroom windows completes the mood of breezy serenity. For furniture, Jackye selected dark wood pieces, including a four-poster bed and rattan-backed campeche chairs that are reminiscent of the décor of Cuban villas. Distressed wood flooring, stained dark brown and covered with a carpet the color of woven grass mats, offers restrained luxury underfoot.

While the bedroom finds a perfect balance between light and shade with its palette of blue, beige, and brown, the master bathroom that opens off of it is as bright as ocean spray. A wall of white marble pierced with clerestory windows admits and reflects the sunlight. A floor of white and gold glass mosaic tile glistens and sparkles like wet seashells kissed by the tide. The large porcelain soaking tub invites restful bathing, while a spacious, plate glass-enclosed shower almost disappears in another corner.

In this master suite, as in the rest of the house, the design team's careful attention to detail, creative use of

Opposite: *Bold textiles with batik-inspired prints add graphic energy to this guest room. Furniture and headboards the color of dark-roasted coffee beans bring to mind the dark mahogany wood favored in traditional Cuban interiors.*

Above: *The mosaic glass tile floor of the master bathroom shimmers like the water's edge. Light from clerestory windows bathes the room without compromising privacy.*

materials, and sensitivity to light and space culminate in beautiful, harmonious rooms that deeply satisfy the senses without clutter or fuss. Simple, durable, timeless materials combine with a relaxed progression of spaces, both enclosed and exposed, to meet the inhabitants' varied needs for sun and shelter, community and retreat. This is the abiding appeal of the Shingle-style house, whether old or new, in New England or on southern shores.

old island style

A LATE-TWENTIETH-CENTURY COTTAGE

Sullivan's Island, South Carolina 〜

Even though this Sullivan's Island home is only a little over fifteen years old, it bears many of the hallmarks of the rustic beach cottages that owner, author Josephine Humphreys, remembers from childhood summers spent on the island in the 1950s. "I heard a man go by with a kid on the back of his bicycle, and he said, 'Now, that's one of the old island houses, that's an original one,'" Jo says gleefully. The house was carefully designed to make it look historic. It's not as big as the newer models, it bears a rusty tin roof, and the old-fashioned dark green they painted it matches the color of Jo's grandfather's house, where she used to spend her summers.

Back then, Jo's entire extended family would pack into the small house bought by her grandfather in 1921 that incorporated parts of a beached boat. "There were hammocks, and swings, and possums in the yard, and electric wires going up the walls and across the ceilings with light bulbs hanging down," she recalls. "I still remember the hand pump at the kitchen sink, which drew rainwater from a cistern in the yard." While today's beachgoers, accustomed to amenities like air conditioning and modern plumbing, might be appalled to find themselves marooned for weeks in such a setting, memories like these loom happily in many a southerner's mind. Jo recalls summers when her grandfather's

Although two stories high now, the main part of the cottage conforms to the outline of the original one-story structure it replaced. An extension to the left accommodates the master bedroom, which has its own porch overlooking the dunes and ocean.

Above: *Collections of flowers and figures made from colorful glass beads; busts and beasts of green-glazed McCoy ware; children's ceramics; and favorite books are displayed to advantage against the dark honey-colored walls of natural pine beadboard.*

Opposite: *Comfortable seating, including French Art Deco club chairs and a pair of rockers reupholstered in vintage curtain fabric, creates an inviting sitting area that parallels the screened porch. Doors and windows open out onto the porch, where louvered shutters made by Tom Hutcheson from a Caribbean design offer protection from the elements.*

beach cottage was packed with family: "My uncle, aunt, and their three children slept in one room, my other uncle and aunt and their three children were in another room, Mama and Daddy and their three children were in another room, and my grandparents had their room."

Eventually, the Humphreys family was able to spread out a bit. Sullivan's Island was one of the few local barrier islands that was growing back then, naturally acquiring beach land as ocean currents brought sand ashore. By the late 1940s, there was enough new land in front of Jo's grandfather's house to accommodate two more lots. Jo's father, William, and his brother drew straws to see who would get the waterfront lot, and her father won. Although the price of five hundred dollars per lot seemed steep at the time, the two brothers bought the properties. In 1957, Jo's mother, Martha, found a model in a magazine for a simple mountain cottage designed by a Japanese architect. She wrote to the architect, asking whether he thought it could withstand hurricane-force winds, and after he responded that he thought it might, Martha and William Humphreys decided to build their new waterfront house according to this plan—a simple one-room box with a slightly inclined roof and a wall of sliding barn doors, with windows facing the Atlantic Ocean.

Jo and her husband, lawyer Tom Hutcheson, bought the tiny, basic house in 1985. When Hurricane Hugo—a category five storm that wreaked massive destruction—lashed Sullivan's Island in 1989, true to the architect's word the tiny square house suffered little except some leaks in the roof. However, the rains that followed the storm, combined with a prolonged evacuation order, resulted in irreparable damage to the

a fish
tale

A TWENTY-FIRST-CENTURY FISH CAMP FANTASY

WaterColor, Florida ⌒⌒

Not that long ago, a summer trip to Florida's panhandle meant serious rustication. Fording rivers on rickety bridges and frog-jumping over bays in ferries, the roads were rough and winding, often petering out before the ultimate destination. But families from Georgia and Alabama have long considered the Gulf Coast's squeaky white sand, translucent emerald waves, and whispering breezes well worth the trip. Even today, the journey feels long, with the final hour spent meandering through sparsely populated woods and farmlands at the back of beyond before the earth falls away to reveal sparkling blue-green waters. Now, however, all the comforts of civilization await, from well-paved streets and air-conditioned interiors to gourmet caffe lattes.

Thirty years ago, little more than scrubby dunes stretched between Panama City and Destin, dotted here and there with unpretentious summer cottages. Today, development is dense along the scenic highway known as 30-A, land values are high, and the architecture is sophisticated and global in its points of reference. While it is easy to find fault with the French- and Mediterranean-style buildings whose scale and materials feel out of place in this elemental setting, the architecture of Seaside, founded in 1980, and its younger neighbor, WaterColor, appears more at home. This is the

While the hipped roof of corrugated metal and center-hall shape is reminiscent of ubiquitous early-twentieth-century southern cottages, the hint of red in the window mullions, tall louvered shutters, and pierced wood detailing on the porch recall Caribbean and Cuban influences.

main body of the house. The only part to survive unscathed was a wraparound deck that Jo and Tom had recently rebuilt.

The couple used the outline of the deck to build a new house with the same footprint as the old one, explaining that they didn't want to waste money tearing the deck down. They expanded out from the previous plan in one corner to accommodate a master bedroom and bath and installed a few new luxuries, including air conditioning and modern electrical wiring. After spending one summer in the house, the two decided not to move back to downtown Charleston in the fall. "We'd always lived in old houses that needed work all the time. It was just magic living in a house where all the plumbing worked and the roof didn't leak," says Jo.

Even though their new house had all the modern comforts, they decided to keep its appearance reminiscent of the relaxed summer lifestyle Jo recalled from her youth. Instead of covering interior surfaces with sheetrock, they used unpainted pine beadboard commonly employed in early-twentieth-century summer cottages. Over time, the pine darkens to a rich brown patina—and it never needs paint. While Jo says they were trying to recapture the feeling of her grandparents' house, she adds, "If you paint, you know you have to repaint."

Tired of formal downtown Charleston living, Jo jettisoned much of her fine wood furniture (what Tom calls "creepy mahogany"), as well as her blue-and-white china, crystal, and silver. "My parents' idea of furnishing their beach house on this same lot was to use things they wouldn't mind losing if the house washed out to sea. I just wanted colorful, funny, cheesy, unfancy things," says Jo. Her overall goal was to have a house that would make children laugh, while at the same time recalling the history and ideas that inspire her writing.

The house does bring a smile, decorated with scenic lamps, colorful beaded glass objects, board games, folk art, and Fiestaware. Jo has been collecting objects for the house for more than fifteen years, among them vintage chenille bedspreads, green-glazed McCoy ware (including a bust of Abraham Lincoln), and cutlery with bakelite handles. A few heirlooms have made their way to the beach house as well, such as Jo's mother's spool bed and matching chest of drawers in the master bedroom and a portrait of Tom's great-grandmother. French Art Deco club chairs add verve to the living room, and French rosewood chairs of the same vintage provide comfortable and stylish seating at the dining room table.

Jo and Tom are both drawn to colorful, quirky folk art that is displayed throughout the house. Their paintings include *I Have a Dream*, a scene in house paint on roofing tin depicting Martin Luther King Jr.'s vision of the sons of slaves and slave owners sitting down together. In South Carolina artist Sam Doyle's interpretation, the children are eating watermelon that, with both black and white seeds, he considered to be an integrated fruit. Jo also likes to collect busts, and among her finds are one of a strange man with a protruding tongue, a Native American head made

When their contractor recommended a cathedral ceiling for this sitting area in the guest quarters, Jo, who prefers the intimacy of low ceilings, suggested using some of the space to accommodate a sleeping loft.

into a lamp, and several other wooden heads that are displayed throughout the rooms. She also appreciates portraits; in a flea market she came across an entire collection of cast-off likenesses, circa 1940, by a single artist, and these now adorn a tall wall in an addition to the house.

Jo and Tom built an extension of the main house to make room for guests, where in addition to welcoming visits from children and grandchildren, they also like to put up artists and scholars. Visitors have their own wing, with a separate entrance and two bedrooms. Even though the house is now quite commodious, with five bedrooms including two on the second floor, and a large office for Jo, it still presents a modest façade, both to the beach and the street. The island has grown so much that the house's beach-front façade, once nearly lapped by high tides, now faces a landscape of dunes and wax myrtles where rabbits play and snakes make their home. The cottage may be relatively new, but it captures the spirit of an old island home where generations have come together to enjoy each other's company at the edge of the sea.

Opposite: *Jo inherited a spool bed and matching dresser from her mother, simple furnishings once commonly found in southern country homes. The shutters dividing the bedroom and dressing area came from an old family house in Summerville, South Carolina.*

Above: *Painted wood furniture, chenille bedspreads, and vintage lighting create an old-fashioned look in a bedroom tucked beneath the roof's gable.*

the ultimate cottage

A 1926 HALL-AND-PARLOR COTTAGE

Grayton Beach, Florida ⤳

If you stand in just the right spot and squint, you can imagine that this weathered cypress cottage is the only structure standing on the wildflower-strewn dunes of Grayton Beach, just as it was in 1926. It is easy to pretend, too, that there is no electricity here, although the brightly colored Christmas lights stringing the front porch are a dead giveaway that this is not the case. Inside, daylight filters in through chinks in the board-and-batten walls and around the edges of shuttered windows. It takes a bit of muscle to open the wooden awning shutters that are hinged at the top and open out, to be propped aloft by cut two-by-fours. But the cool breezes that sweep in through the screens (also hinged at the top, but opening inward) quickly dry any sweat worked up in the process and prove how comfortable this simple cottage was, and still is, without modern air conditioning.

Owner Lee Burdett is a descendent of the Lee family that has summered in the house since 1938. In the 1950s, she began spending summers at the cottage with her grandmother, Ethel Lee, who bought it from the original owner in 1938. Back then no road led directly to the cabin; Lee and her grandmother had to walk from the main road, hauling all their summer gear and provisions, which included several live chickens. Everything about the trip was an adventure, recalls Lee, including

The Butler cottage is raised several feet above the sand, inviting cool ocean breezes to flow beneath the floorboards.

the fact that the landscape around the cottage changed each year: "Sometimes the sand dunes would be almost all the way up to the porch. Other times, we could hang a hammock beneath the house and see the Gulf from the windows."

While nature is still a potent force for change along the Gulf Coast of the Florida panhandle, population growth, skyrocketing land values, and new architecture and lifestyle trends pose greater threats to this and the other modest cottages of Grayton Beach. "It used to be you'd put up the shutters and see the dunes forever," recalls Lee. Not so anymore: the development of the area is a typical story of success gone out of control, with larger and larger houses replacing many original cottages and crowding the beach front.

In the early decades of the nineteenth century, a small seasonal community for families from nearby DeFuniak Springs and Chipley sprang up, comprised of one- and two-room shacks with verandas and kitchen wings. The original owner of the cottage, Van Butler, first came to the remote Gulf Coast outpost with his father in 1911, at the age of eight. According to a history of the town prepared by the Coastal Heritage Preservation Foundation, "the trip to the beach took an indirect route over rough roads in a Model T, . . . involved a river crossing at Cow Ford on the Choctawhatchee River, . . . and took nearly all day."

The front door of the cottage opens into a room the family calls "the porch," which is furnished simply with iron beds and homemade furniture. Doors and windows pierce the long interior wall, offering cooling air circulation as well as access to the house's two other rooms.

By 1919, Grayton Beach's reputation as a bathing resort had spread far enough to attract the attention of a group of midwesterners who conceived, but never completed, a plan to develop the Iowa Grayton Beach Club. Development instead fell to a group of Floridians, spearheaded by Butler's father, who promoted lots for sale among fellow southerners, rehabilitated older cottages as rentals, and built a hotel. Butler joined the family dynasty in 1926, homesteading an eighty-acre tract known as New Grayton Beach and staking his claim with this simple cypress cottage that still stands. Considered the unofficial mayor of Grayton Beach, he opened a store in what was to become the downtown area in the 1930s. But it was more than a store to this community, explains Lee's aunt, Teresa Ray, whose sister (Lee's mother) met her husband there: "It was the place where everybody gathered at night. There was a jukebox, and everybody danced. The mothers would sit around and watch, and sometimes they would dance, too."

What the family couldn't buy at the store, they fished from nearby waters or purchased from local farms. "You could go out and get a bucket full of crabs," says Teresa, describing mouthwatering meals of gumbo and stuffed shellfish. The local waters also provided constant entertainment. "We got up and swept the house every morning," Teresa continues, adding with a laugh, "that was about all you could do to it. Then we got to the beach as soon as we could and stayed out there practically all day. After dark, we'd do our hair, dress, and get ready to go to the store."

The same outdoor shower that served Teresa and her four sisters still provides the only bathing facilities at the cottage, which is now used by Lee and her

children as well as other family members. Lee remembers racing her brothers back to the house to get the first rush of sun-warmed water, before the hot-water heater was installed. While Teresa's reminiscences include a great ball of fire running across the floor of the house during a thunderstorm, Lee's feature a skunk strolling beneath the house and a litter of wild boar piglets she discovered in a clearing.

Today, the rough boards lining the interior of the house seem saturated with the memories of a hundred happy summers. It is easy to imagine a house full of grown-ups and children swapping stories as they pile into the iron bedsteads arranged in the combined living and sleeping area running the length of the house and the other bedroom; or to envision them cooking, eating, and playing board games or cards in the third room, a kitchen and dining area simply furnished with a homemade picnic table and two long benches.

Family members call the long room that parallels the bedroom and kitchen "the porch," though it may have been enclosed when Butler built the house. Certainly, its many screened windows lend it an airy, porchlike atmosphere. "My grandmother always called her bedroom in Montgomery,

There is no interior siding on the cypress walls. Long vertical cracks in them provide nearly as much ventilation as the unglazed windows, which can be closed by removing the two-by-fours that prop open the awning shutters. The pitched roof allows hot air to rise above the rooms, which are also cooled by breezes flowing beneath (and between) the floorboards.

Alabama the 'sleeping porch,'" explains Lee, "so it may just be a Southern thing." In fact, many southern sleeping porches are actually fully enclosed rooms with plentiful windows on three sides to promote cross-ventilation.

The arrangement of rooms in the cottage is reminiscent of a dwelling type known as a hall-and-parlor house, found first in America in the Plymouth colony and dating back to medieval England and Wales. Traditionally, these dwellings had two side-by-side entrances, one into the "hall," which functioned as the cooking, dining, and gathering space, and one into the "parlor," a private room used primarily for sleeping. In this fashion, the cottage has doors and windows from both rooms opening onto "the porch," which stands where a traditional hall-and-parlor house's open-air porch would have been. It is interesting to consider that an aspect of this ancient house form—the combined kitchen/dining/living room, now called a "great room"—has become popular again after many centuries.

While Grayton Beach is fortunate to retain twenty or so historic cottages that preserve the area's architectural past, their number is shrinking as large new houses are built in their place. "The cottage definitely has a lot of age on it," says Teresa, who confesses that she and her sisters, who co-own it, worry about fire, which is why they don't rent it out, despite numerous inquiries. "I can't tell you how much we love the cabin," adds Lee. "We are holding on by our fingernails."

Above: *An old pump handle is evidence of how water was once delivered to the kitchen sink. A modern stove and refrigerator have replaced the old wood-burning stove and icebox that Teresa Ray remembers her mother using.*

Opposite: *At the Butler cottage, a shallow shed roof extends from a steeper gable to cover an enclosed sleeping porch. The cottage's walls and awning shutters (so called because they open out over the unglazed windows like awnings) are constructed of local cypress applied in the board-and-batten style.*

palm cottage

A RESCUED 1920S BEACH COTTAGE

Tybee Island, Georgia ⌒

Georgia's Tybee Island is the kind of beach community that inspires not just a lazy summer love, but a deep and abiding passion. While plenty of newcomers see its old cottages as "tear-downs," many diehard old-timers will go to almost any length to save even the most humble historic dwelling. Jane Coslick is one of these, a native of nearby Savannah who grew up escaping the summer heat on Tybee. "People used to move down here for the whole summer in the days before air conditioning," recalls Jane, who began her campaign to preserve the island's historic structures by rescuing this lovely 1920s cottage.

People from all over Georgia and beyond have long come to enjoy Tybee's fresh breezes. By the late nineteenth century, it was a popular destination for sufferers of asthma, allergies, and other respiratory disorders who came to "take the salts." Pleasure seekers took a ferry to the island's shores to stroll the beaches or enjoy the view from the elegant arcades of the Tybee Hotel and DeSoto Beach Hotel, both now gone. The Tybrisa Pavilion was a center of social life, with its crystal ball, live music, and dime dances. By the early twentieth century, the Central of Georgia Railway had built a spur connecting Tybee to the mainland, making the trip easier for tourists

French doors open from the living room onto the porch's outdoor living space.
Jane Coslick gave the house her trademark look, painting the interior walls white
and adding bright shots of color, like this chartreuse door surround.

Above: *As the first of many cottages rescued by Jane, Palm Cottage bears a hand-painted historic marker that the preservationist hopes will encourage similar restoration efforts.*

Opposite: *When Palm Cottage was constructed in the 1920s, it had only two rooms. The front porch was later enclosed to accommodate a second bedroom and a side porch was added. Original board-and-batten shutters decorated with a palm motif inspired its name.*

Overleaf: *The screened porch creates a large indoor-outdoor living area that is current owner Susan Lowrey Flaherty's favorite place to read, rest, and entertain. It also allows her to leave doors open to increase the flow of air through the house, which she rarely air-conditions.*

from all over the state, and by 1923, a road offered even better access.

This six-hundred-square-foot cottage that Jane rescued from demolition in 1998 dates from the road-building era, when the U.S. Army Corps of Engineers constructed a number of simple dwellings for its workers. Jane was living in one of them when she was distressed to learn that the neighboring house, which she later named Palm Cottage, was to be demolished by its owners. She tried to convince them that it was worth restoring, and even offered her design services for free. The owners turned her down, but proposed selling the house for a dollar if she would move it to a new site. She agreed. Upset by the demolition of so many local structures, ranging from modest cottages to historic hotels, Jane was determined to rescue this little bit of history.

At the time, Palm Cottage—named for the silhouettes of palm trees that decorate its board-and-batten shutters—was not so lovely to look at, and neighbors complained as it sat for a year on the lot to which it was moved. Unable to sell the houses, Jane decided to restore it in order to demonstrate how charming such a cottage could be. Fortunately, it was in good condition, with much of the original material and details remaining. Although the front porch had been enclosed to create an additional room, the original pocket windows were still intact. Jane left them to enhance airflow and also as a reminder of the original shape of the house. "I thought the front room might not be so nice," Jane recalls. "But I discovered that it is such a cozy space for reading and sleeping."

WELCOME!!
to the
BEACH!
Have Fun & come
on BACK!

When Jane bought the cottage, the back bedroom, with its low, sloping ceiling and unattractive windows installed by previous owners, was not inviting. Jane had the ceiling raised and leveled, and installed casement windows with transoms above to create an airy master bedroom. The completed cottage also includes a spacious side porch, one-and-a-half baths, an indoor laundry room, and a brightly painted outdoor shower —something that has become a signature element in many of the cottages Jane has restored on Tybee.

Jane spared no expense on this house, and the restored cottage quickly sold to a couple who discovered it while bicycling past on their way to breakfast. It has since been featured in both national and local publications. Current owner Susan Lowrey Flaherty first saw it during a visit to a friend on Tybee, and was immediately smitten. It came up for sale twice but was snapped up both times before she could buy it. When the cottage came on the market again in 2002, Susan made an offer, determined not to miss it again. The offer was accepted on Christmas Eve, when her realtor called and said, "Merry Christmas, the cottage is yours."

Susan, a resident of Savannah, has been living part-time in the cottage for four years. Among the features she cherishes, she lists: "The intimacy, the windows with the transoms, the fact that you can open every window and get this wonderful cross-ventilation and let the outside in. I love the way it's nestled into the rustling palm trees and pines. I watch the raccoons roaming the yard and climbing the trees." Like Jane, who wants to share the Tybee Island that she grew up loving with future generations, Susan is also generous with her cottage. She rents it out for several months of the year, not just for the income, but so that other people can have the experience. Tybee was always filled with simple, old beach houses, but that is changing with a lot of the new construction. Susan wants people to discover the pleasures of living in a simple, old cottage, lulled by the sound of the surf and the ocean's breezes.

Although change is in the air at Tybee, many people are working hard to preserve a bit of the past. Committed to preserving the whole island, Jane continues to buy and restore several cottages each year. "People have been moving these cottages from place to place on the island for at least a century," she explains, indicating her own house, which was relocated by barge from its previous location. "An old house has so much more energy, more passion, and more comfort than a new one."

Once an exterior wall, the wall dividing the living room from the front bedroom includes original pocket windows that open up into recesses above the window frames. Painted beadboard covers the walls and ceilings of the bedroom that was originally a sleeping porch.

Opposite: *With windows in all four walls and a sloping roof, this guest bedroom retains the airy character of an old sleeping porch.*

Above: *A large living, dining, and kitchen area fills the front half of the house. With windows, transoms, and doors that open on three sides, the room is filled with light and sea breezes.*

past
present

A STORY-AND-A-JUMP IN OCRACOKE VILLAGE

Ocracoke Island, North Carolina ⌒

Ocracoke Island is one of those increasingly rare places in the United States that seems to have sidestepped the passage of time. There are a few modern incursions impossible to ignore, including a two-lane highway bisecting the sixteen-mile-long island that bustles with traffic during the summer resort season. But if you turn off this road onto one of the sandy paths that zigzag through a canopy of scrub trees, small white houses, and ancient cemeteries, you enter the timeless world of Ocracoke Village.

Ocracoke Island was named after the Native Americans who once inhabited the small island off the coast of North Carolina. English settlers arrived in the early eighteenth century, and the island changed hands several times before William Howard, its fourth owner, bought it in 1759 for 105 pounds sterling. Howard's descendents have since thrived on the island for ten generations, making many contributions to its history.

Howard Street is one of the oldest and best preserved of the old sand roads in Ocracoke Village, a settlement on the western side of the island with a population of approximately 650 year-round residents. It borders a plot of land still in Howard family hands, with several buildings, including a

The façade of Philip Howard's circa 1865 story-and-a-jump cottage is almost
exactly as it was when his grandparents moved in during the late nineteenth century.
The only major change is the small bathroom addition on the right.

gallery called Village Craftsmen, owned by Philip Howard, William's eighth-generation descendent. Although Philip grew up near Philadelphia, where many Ocracokers moved in the mid-twentieth century to find work, thirty years ago he returned to make his home on the island. A gallery owner and artist (his pen-and-ink drawings of Ocracoke scenes are popular items in the gallery's inventory of arts and crafts), Philip's vocation seems to be that of unofficial village historian—a natural role for one whose family has practically sprung from the island's soil.

At home, Philip surrounds himself with many historic artifacts that have come down through his family, but the house itself is the greatest of all the relics that this Ocracoker has cared for and preserved. Built circa 1865 and moved to its present location on a path off of Howard Street in 1893, the house has been in Philip's family for three generations. His great-grand-parents gave it as a wedding gift to his grandparents, Homer and Aliph Howard, whom Philip visited regularly on summers away from Philadelphia. He remembers sitting on their "pizer," as Ocrockers call porches in their unique dialect (it is a corruption of the word "piazza," which English colonialists used for "porch"), and enjoying dinners of old drum in the small dining room. Consisting of layers of boiled pota-toes; flaked, boiled drum (a local fish); chopped onion; boiled egg; and rendered salt pork drizzled with vine-gar and pork drippings, the dish, which Philip describes as "more a ritual than a meal," is another vestige of

A small window set beneath the angle of the porch's shed roof opens into the second-floor bedroom. This is a distinctive feature of eastern North Carolina's story-and-a-jump cottages.

old Ocracoke. "Never plan anything after eating this," advise the authors of the *Ocracoke Cook Book* (avail-able at Village Craftsmen and the Ocracoke Preservation Society Museum). "Just slide under the table and rest a spell."

The house is built in a form called a story-and-a-jump that was popular (and practical) in Ocracoke and other parts of eastern North Carolina in the eigh-teenth and nineteenth centuries. The name refers to a one-and-a-half story house—the "jump" being the half-story beneath the gabled roof. The roof is sup-ported by a wall approximately three feet high built atop the ceiling joists of the first floor, which elevates the roof sufficiently to accommodate a standing-room ceiling below. This wall also contains two (or some-times three) small windows that open beneath a shed roof sheltering the front porch. Larger windows pierce the gable ends of the house, providing airflow from three sides, which was essential during the days when sea breezes were the only means of cooling off during the area's hot, muggy summers.

It's hard to imagine Homer and Aliph raising eight children in the small four-room dwelling, but Ocracokers were accustomed to living in small houses. Wood was scarce on the island, which is covered with scrub trees too small to produce building material. Timbers from wrecked ships were commonly used for construction, and the Howard house boasts some of these. When Philip bought the house in 1990 (it had passed briefly out of Howard hands in the mid-twentieth century) and began restoring it several years later, he discovered ship's knees (sturdy, hand-hewn right-angle joints) used as braces, timbers functioning as floor and ceiling joists, and brass hardware with a distinctly maritime appearance.

The house was badly in need of repair by the time Philip began his restoration with the goal of returning the cottage to its mid-nineteenth-century appearance. In time-honored Ocracoke fashion, Philip salvaged additional material from another house of the same age to replace rotting windows and floorboards. Rather than replace the deteriorating porch posts, Philip had new wood spliced onto the bottom of the original posts using wooden pegs. He reused all the original floorboards that could be saved, numbering them and returning them to their proper place after restabilizing the support beams beneath them.

The eighteen-month-long project turned up a corner post of the old back porch that was enclosed to accommodate the kitchen in the 1930s. This item played an important role in Philip's decision to paint the cottage's exterior trim red. "My dad always told me that his mother wanted her husband to paint the trim red, and that he never would," recalls Philip. "As long as we could remember, it had always been green or white. I thought that I might like to paint the trim red, just for grandmother Aliph." When he discovered the original porch post in the back, he realized it must have been that color at some point during her lifetime, but no one remembered it. He tried to match the color as closely as possible.

There are other links to history contained in this venerable house. "My great-grandfather was the first keeper of the life-saving station that used to be on the north end of the island," says Philip, who has kept some of James Howard's hand-penned logs that record wrecks and rescues from 1883 to the early 1900s. Another prized possession is a Victorian rocking chair that was salvaged from a British steamship wrecked off the island's coast. In gratitude for saving

Opposite: *A Victorian rocker salvaged from a wreck and given to Philip's great-grandfather flanks the parlor fireplace, along with a reproduction of it made from driftwood by Philip's father. A photograph of Aliph and Homer Howard hangs on the wall, and a ship's knee balances on the mantel.*

Above: *An antique pocket watch was a gift from Philip's companion, Lou Ann Homan, who shares his passion for history. It sits upon the pages of a log written by Philip's great-grandfather, who was the keeper of Ocracoke's life-saving station.*

Above: *Originally, the house's kitchen was located in a separate building. In the 1930s, a back porch was enclosed to accommodate this kitchen and dining area. Philip found the plank table with turned legs in the house when he purchased it; the iron chandelier and pierced tin sconces were made by craftsmen who supply his gallery.*

Opposite: *Philip remembers sleeping in this room as a boy. He and Lou Ann found most of the first-floor bedroom's simple furnishings and quilt at antiques stores and auctions. Family photographs adorn the wall and desk.*

his life and that of eight other passengers and crew, the ship's captain gave Keeper Howard the chair. A near-reproduction of this chair, made by Philip's father entirely from wood that drifted ashore, an old photograph of his grandparents in an oval frame with domed glass, and several duck decoys carved and painted by both close and distant relatives are also among the house's treasures.

On a recent stormy night, Philip and his companion, Lou Ann Homan, who divides her time between Indiana and Ocracoke, sat in the parlor telling ghost stories to visitors who signed up for one of the tours offered throughout the summer season. Because of the blustery weather, that night's walking tour was canceled and the guests were invited to sit in the Howard house's parlor as the pair regaled them with stories by the light of candles and kerosene lanterns. Philip told several hair-raising tales of island ghosts while Lou Ann, a professional storyteller, related a number of otherworldly seafaring accounts. A woman leapt from her rocking chair when Lou Ann told of its origins on a wrecked ship where most of the passengers perished.

But the present is as rich as the past in this timeless cottage. Philip makes fig cake in his grandmother's kitchen, a favorite island recipe inspired by the copious fig trees that flourish in the sandy soil. He and Lou Ann sit on the pizer's porch swing and enjoy the morning and evening breezes. And they walk to work at Philip's gallery, sometimes barefooted, on the path that cuts through old Howard property. "I sit on the pizer every morning sipping my coffee," says Lou Ann. "I don't wear a watch, so I don't know what time it is. When the church bells chime at nine o'clock, I put my coffee down and walk to work. I'm there by the ninth chime."

Opposite: *A narrow staircase leads to the second-floor bedroom. Philip painted it a shade of hunter green popular on the island.*

Above: *The second-floor bedroom reveals the characteristic knee-wall and small floor-level windows of the story-and-a-jump form. The floor originally housed two bedrooms, but Philip reconfigured it to include one spacious bedroom and bathroom. The quilt on the bed was sewn by Lou Ann's great-grandmother.*

island harmony

A CONCH COTTAGE, CIRCA 1896

Key West, Florida ～

The old-world charm and tropical beauty of Key West is a delightful surprise at the end of Highway 1, the two-lane road that cuts a swath through the primitive landscape and touristy sprawl of the Florida Keys. Chock-a-block with tiny cottages and larger houses wrapped with porches, the old town's maze of streets is a house lover's dream. It seems almost impossible that so many styles—Bahamian, Italianate, Greek Revival, Queen Anne, and Arts and Crafts—could coexist so densely and happily in such a remote and storm-prone outpost. And yet, they do.

Ninety miles north of Cuba, the island accommodates the United States' southernmost international port, and the variety of its architectural styles speaks of its historic development. In the early nineteenth century, sea captains from New England built houses here with double-hung sash windows and widows' walks reminiscent of their northern home. Salvaging cargo from ships wrecked on nearby coral reefs was also a primary source of income here in the nineteenth century, drawing "wreckers" from the nearby Bahamas who in turn imported their own architectural traditions. The growth of the cigar-making industry in the nineteenth century brought an influx of Cuban workers,

With its long, single-file series of rooms opening off a narrow hall and running the length of the house, George Davis' circa 1896 conch cottage is a typical cigar maker's house. This enfilade arrangement of rooms not only encourages cross-ventilation, but also makes it possible to squeeze several of the narrow cottages on a small plot of land.

Above: *Owner George Davis transformed the side yard into an inviting outdoor space featuring a soft sand-colored stone pool patio encircled by tropical plants. The cottage's typical tin roof deflects the sun's heat, while the narrow porch provides a barrier of shade.*

Opposite: *A glossy, pale gray glaze brightens the walls of the living room, and the dark brown floor seems to recede, creating an illusion of greater space. A French kneehole desk covered in rattan and an antique English pot rack holding large conch shells add summery notes of style.*

who contributed further to the West Indian appearance of the local architecture. Southern interests in the port brought Greek Revival design in the mid-nineteenth century, and continued prosperity witnessed the construction of many homes in Victorian styles. By 1912, hotel and railroad entrepreneur Henry Flagler succeeded in connecting Key West by rail to the mainland, thus establishing the link that led to its present-day popularity as a vacation destination.

The houses that this diverse population built include both conch cottages, as the one-room-wide

Above: *An English Regency table of bamboo and lacquer boasts a collection of turtle shells and turtle-inspired decorative objects in the living room.*

Opposite: *A breezeway like space at the back of the house accommodates a tiny dining room that overlooks the pool terrace. This airy room provides just enough space for a dining table set with Wedgwood's Nantucket Basket china, designed by George.*

dwellings built for cigar-making families are known, and gracious center-hall houses with spacious rooms and wide verandas. The influx of Bahamian and Cuban immigrants brought a distinctly tropical feel to the local buildings, which borrowed sensible island-born elements including raised pier foundations, wide porches, second-floor balconies, louvered shutters, and roofs covered with sun-deflecting tin. Surrounded by

dense tropical flora, these houses make the most of the naturally cooling elements of breeze and shade. In addition, the nineteenth- and early-twentieth-century styles and forms brought by New Englanders and southerners were modified to function efficiently in the sultry climate, acquiring porches, shutters, and tin roofs that visually unite them.

Most of the houses are constructed of Dade County pine that was shipped from the Florida mainland. While interior walls are often allowed to darken naturally to a deep reddish brown, the exteriors are typically painted white or pastel shades. Pine is also widely used for flooring, although large terracotta squares of easily imported Cuban tile are another common material. While grander houses boast elegant interior details, the Bahamian-style houses and conch cottages are sparer. Decorative detail without is provided by simple cutouts of geometric or plant motifs in flat boards that serve as balusters on porches, fence palings, or board-and-batten shutters—the latter often painted in bright tropical tones.

The architectural environment that results from the marriage of these factors offers an immense variety of form and style within a limited scale and palette of materials. Add to it the exuberance of the tropical foliage—rustling palm trees, bright hibiscus and bougainvillea, and giant elephant ears—and Key West becomes one of the most romantic and exotic destinations in the United States. And this is what drew designer George Davis to its historic streets, where he eventually found this lovely cottage. A peripatetic man, George has called many places home, among them Aspen, Diamond Head, Hawaii, and Nantucket. "I have moved to these places because I

love them," he explains. "I need to wake up in the morning and see something inspiring. I like towns with history. My environment is eighty percent of my life."

For the last forty years, George has lived year-round or summered on Nantucket, where he operates a shop called Weeds that features English and continental European antiques. This venture marks only the most recent episode in a varied career during which he also operated Nantucket's first surf shop, and worked as a fine artist, decorative painter, art dealer, and interior designer. Among his most successful professional ventures is a foray into tableware design, which resulted in the creation of a popular white china pattern produced by Wedgwood called Nantucket Basket.

For ten years of his residence on Nantucket, George escaped the cold Atlantic winters to Hawaii, but one year he decided to winter in Key West instead, renting a friend's cottage and exploring the island. On a rainy-day whim, he called a realtor to show him around. The first house he saw was a rundown conch cottage just a half block off Duval Street, the old town's busy commercial boulevard. Tiny and neglected, the house had been badly subdivided into apartments, and its overgrown garden was brimming with stray cats and chickens. But to George, the house looked like it belonged in Hawaii, with all its vines and tropical plants; all it needed, he says, was "some tender, loving care." George admits to questioning his own impulse after he bought the cottage, "but ultimately," he concludes, "it turned out to be exactly what I was looking for."

A contemporary pot stand of stainless steel is a replica of an antique design popular in English kitchens. Its space-saving obelisk shape adds a decorative as well as utilitarian element to the cottage's tiny kitchen.

Built around 1896, the house is a typical cigar maker's cottage. Like the shotgun cottages of New Orleans (also influenced by the architecture of the Caribbean), these structures are narrow, single-story houses with a series of rooms opening in an enfilade (or single-file) arrangement from one into the next. A porch parallels the rooms, opening onto a side yard which in this case was strictly utilitarian, originally including a chicken coop and cistern. Now the small rectangle of space is devoted to leisure, with an elegant marble-topped pool patio surrounded by verdant foliage.

With only one thousand square feet of interior space to work with, George and his contractor devised a surprisingly hospitable suite of rooms, including a living room, dining area, kitchen, two bedrooms, and two baths. By glazing the pine walls a pale shade of gray and keeping furnishings simple and to scale, George has created an impression of airiness that offsets the rooms' diminutive size. A tiny pair of French rattan-and-bamboo side tables offers small-scale storage in the master bedroom, which also includes vintage bamboo furniture from Key West. A louvered screen (originally a vent from a barn in Maine) forms a rustic headboard for the bed, its large scale somehow making the small room appear grander than it is.

George plays a similar game of scale in the guest room, creating a tall headpiece with a French Chippendale-style canopy that he found in London. Painted white and draped with blue-and-white toile, the canopy hovers like a giant cloud above the bed. More white-painted furnishings complete the room's décor, including a Gothic-arched window frame backed with mirror.

Above: *George's small bedroom includes elements from many of his favorite places, such as a Hawaiian* pareau *textile tucked across the pillows, an English Drabware pitcher perched on a bamboo shelf, and a barn vent from New England that brings to mind the louvered shutters favored in Key West.*

Opposite: *The guest bedroom's white furniture and blue-and-white toile draperies combine for a serenely elegant setting. George fashioned the fanciful canopy from pieces of French Chippendale-style furniture that he purchased in England.*

By using space-saving devices, such as refrigerated drawer units and a diminutive dishwasher, George squeezed the maximum amount of utility into the tiny kitchen that opens off a hallway-cum-dining room leading to the side porch. An obelisk-shaped pot stand of stainless steel, designed after traditional English versions, creates a vertical element in the space while providing ingenious storage space.

Another antique pot stand occupies the living room, but this one holds shells. In this largest of the rooms, George employs another inventive technique to invoke the illusion of space: by painting the floor a deep shade of brownish-black, he causes it to visually recede, at the same time lending a dramatic background to the room's bamboo furniture and Donghia textiles with turtle motifs. While the fabric recalls the local fauna of sea turtles, the finest piece of furniture in the room, an English Regency table of black lacquer and bamboo, injects a note of transatlantic elegance. Locally found accoutrements, such as a voodoo head with cowrie-shell eyes and vintage postcards, bring the décor back to the island.

Taken as a whole, the interior's blend of refinement and tropical relaxation reflect George's wandering eye for style. When he's not shopping in Brighton or London for antiques to sell in his Nantucket store, he's exploring the flea markets and vintage shops of Key West for exotica. Both seem at home in this southernmost outpost of the United States, where George finds "a certain kind of elegant squalor or genteel decrepitude that appeals to me." Here, people are less uptight about style and there is a feeling of homeliness; fabrics get faded in the sun, and the furniture gets a bit less elbow-grease. To George, this speaks of the relaxed pace of the islands. "In Palm Beach, all those chickens would get murdered in a minute," he notes. "Here, everybody is living in some kind of strange harmony with the chickens, the cats, and the geckos."

country

retreats

little charleston of the mountains

A VICTORIAN CENTER-HALL COTTAGE

Flat Rock, North Carolina ⁓

The cool breezes, luminous lakes, and gentle mountain landscape of Flat Rock, North Carolina, have long attracted families from Charleston and other historic plantation settlements in South Carolina who sought to escape summer's heat and diseases. Known as the "Little Charleston of the Mountains," Flat Rock is located southeast of Asheville, not far from the South Carolina border, and just high enough in the Blue Ridge Mountains to provide a desirable change of air. South Carolinians have been building summer homes there since the early nineteenth century, many in the manner of English country houses. In fact, Flat Rock's first great estate was built in 1827 by an Englishman named Charles Baring, a partner of London's Baring Brothers & Company banking firm.

The house that Charlestonian Marty Whaley Adams Cornwell and her husband, Charles, call their summer home dates from just after the Civil War. Marty came into possession of the charming Victorian center-hall cottage twenty-four years ago, through a combination of chance and her family's commitment to preservation. In the 1970s, she received a call from Historic Flat Rock informing her that a house had been donated to the organization with the goal of raising money for a revolving

Delicate tracery in sheer red and bronze decorates the walls of the library and the master bedroom, evoking eighteenth- and nineteenth-century Swedish style.

fund to support preservation of the town's endangered historic houses. Marty and her first husband were invited to purchase it partly because the original owner, a Mr. Elliott, had bequeathed his watch fob to a cousin of Marty's grandfather. The offer may also have had something to do with the fact that Marty's father, Ben Scott Whaley, had helped to establish a similar revolving fund to protect Charleston's historic architecture.

When Marty went to see the house, the custodian was unable to produce the keys to the property, so her first views of the interior were limited to tantalizing glimpses through the windows and French doors. But the quiet dignity of the cottage, which is situated atop a hill covered with hemlock and overlooking a greensward that rolls gently down toward a lake, and its inviting porches and pretty Victorian detailing captured her imagination. The young couple decided to take it, and Marty says, "I've never regretted it, I'll tell you that."

The house has long exerted a kind of enchantment upon those who encounter it. Marty attributes the house's survival to a couple named the Hartmans, who bought it during World War II. Residents of Detroit, they were passing through Flat Rock on their way to

While dark mahogany Victorian furniture lends an American style to the dining room, Marty's wall treatments, including delicate stenciling and montage, and the grisaille-glazed mirrors are reminiscent of Swedish country houses.

Overleaf: *The wide center hall with doors at both ends invites air to flow through the house, naturally cooling the rooms. French doors open off the front porch into two rooms for entertaining.*

winter in Florida when they ran out of gas and gas coupons. Temporarily stranded, they explored the town and its surroundings, and the wife discovered a neglected Victorian house overlooking a lake that captivated her. The Hartmans eventually continued on to Florida, but the following year Mrs. Hartman told her husband that she had to see the house again. The couple returned to Flat Rock and bought it, rescuing the cottage from neglect and restoring it as their winter home. When they finally decided to give it up, they donated it to Historic Flat Rock in support of a local effort to protect the town's old homes and old-fashioned lifestyle.

When Marty came into possession of the two-story house, it had two parlors flanking a wide center hall, a dining room, a kitchen in a shed roof addition, four bedrooms, and three 1940s-era bathrooms. She did little to this original structure, except to transform one of the parlors into a dining room, turn the former dining room into the kitchen, and create a large pantry of the previous kitchen. Since then, the cottage has been

Above left: *A bit of old wallpaper is still visible in a corner of the second-floor space that Marty transformed into a library for Charles. A palette of beige, bronze, and red offers a masculine note without diminishing the hall's airy atmosphere.*

Left: *A bamboo screen adds natural tone and texture to the nearly all-white master bedroom, furnished with Victorian furniture painted in high-gloss white.*

Opposite: *Paintings by Marty's mother, well-known gardener and author Emily Whaley, hang on the wall in the dining room. Hydrangeas from the garden that Marty and her mother planted make perfect bouquets for the room's relaxed elegance.*

enjoyed each summer by her mother, Emily Whaley (author of *Mrs. Whaley and Her Charleston Garden*), and her sisters, children, and second husband Charles, along with a slew of visiting cousins, nieces, nephews, and friends. "My mother and I created a vision for this house as a place where people come to write, paint, or just generate inspiration for creativity," she says. An artist herself, Marty spends hours here each summer painting, while Charles reads and edits manuscripts. Marty's mother wrote two books there (both the afore-mentioned best-selling garden memoir and its sequel, *Mrs. Whaley Entertains*), and also played piano in the parlor; upon her death in 1998, she left her share in the house to Marty's sister, Emily Whipple.

While Marty's primary artistic mediums are watercolor, oil, and monotype, she also excels in the decorative arts, so it is no surprise that she has trans-formed this summer getaway into a hand-decorated country seat for inspirational living. The creative energy and handmade beauty of the rooms recalls that of the English country house known as Charleston, the rural retreat from London for the artists and intellectuals of the Bloomsbury Group. "I like homemade things," Marty states. "I don't like the idea of getting a profes-sional and making the house so perfect that you rob it of all its character, so you don't know who owns it. A house doesn't tell you anything about the owners unless you have something in it that is homemade."

Marty's watercolors, vintage family photographs, and a Victorian daybed from an old family home create a sense of intimacy in the guest room. Inspired by the look of hand-decorated bedding in Swedish interiors, Marty sewed together old cross-stitched placemats that belonged to a great-aunt to make the padded headboard and throw cushions.

A whimsical birdhouse and white-painted metal chairs are bright highlights amid the garden's abundant foliage.

The house's interior walls are covered in plaster containing a large amount of lime, which renders them difficult to paint in conventional ways and thus invites creative flair. Marty, who studied decorative painting in Atlanta, says that while she will never give up fine art painting, sometimes she will take a break from that work to go and plaster a room or stencil. As a result, the wall surfaces in all the rooms are delightfully varied and whimsical.

In the dining room, Marty painted the walls softly variegated shades of beige with bright white cornice and window surrounds stenciled in abstract foliage patterns. Copies of family engravings—sepia-toned silhouettes of ancestors—are integrated into the design, and watercolors of the local scenery painted by Marty's mother hang on the walls. Furniture from old family homes in South Carolina fills the room; an old dining table from Gippy Plantation occupies the niche created by a bay window, and wonderfully knobby Victorian chairs populate the corners. A hand-painted table created by a friend, Marty's framer, the late Hector Dewart, sits in the center of the room, offering the perfect gathering place for long lunchtime or dinner conversations. Dinners here start late, and often feature fresh vegetables and fruit from the farmer's market in nearby Hendersonville. Candlelight turns the walls a deep flickering gold, and the French doors that open onto the porch allow for gentle breezes.

The house's two entertaining rooms, separated by a wide stair hall, provide plenty of space for large parties—including a wedding reception several years ago when Marty and Charles were married just down the hill in the historic St. John in the Wilderness Church (formerly Charles Baring's private chapel). "The house is at its best when it is full of people, sitting on the porches, reading, writing, painting, or playing music," says Marty.

The front porch functions as Marty's summer painting studio, and is also Charles' favorite spot to work, in a corner that commands a view of the lake. "I can sit on the porch with a book in front of me and focus on what I'm doing, and then look up and see this marvelous view," he says. "I get quite out of sorts on rainy days when I can't sit out there." When the weather doesn't cooperate, Charles retreats to the library to work. Before Marty transformed the wide second-floor hallway into the library, it was a wasted space that attracted clutter and little else. Several large wooden bookshelves that once belonged to a public school were painted white with a rich red backing. Taking a cue from Swedish design, she glazed and stenciled the shelves, transforming them from functional to fanciful. They fit the space perfectly, storing a collection of books from Charles' teaching days at Davidson College in North Carolina. Marty painted the walls pale beige and chalky white, and then stenciled delicate garlands, bellflowers, and other old-world motifs on the walls and ceilings in shades of bronzed umber and red. Arts and Crafts–style brass lamps that came from Charles' grandmother's house in Lattimore, North Carolina, illuminate the space.

Marty has always loved the way Swedish country houses capture the light and their beautiful details. While her bright and breezy summer house doesn't need much help in the former area, she has followed the Swedish attention to surface detail in the downstairs bedroom, where stenciled leaf patterns cover the walls and handsewn cross-stitching decorates the bedding. A variety of fabrics add glimpses of color and pattern to the predominantly white room, and includes a block-printed Indian fabric lining a canopy that Marty created to bestow a hint of luxury.

When not painting on the porch, decorating rooms, or entertaining friends, Marty might be found in the garden beside the house. She and her mother began it seventeen years ago. "It started out as a small circle, and it just kept growing," laughs Marty, an accomplished gardener who writes a gardening column for the local Charleston newspaper. Overall, Marty says that the mood she strives to create in the cottage is a relaxed environment that stimulates the imagination. "I want people to leave this house feeling like they can do it, too," says Marty, referring to artistic self-expression. "I hope that it will always be a catalyst, in a very calm way, to help others find their inner sources of creativity."

evolving landscape

A CONVERTED NINETEENTH-CENTURY COTTON GIN HOUSE

Wadmalaw Island, South Carolina ∼

"My life was short on nature," says Trenholm Walker, recalling a time twenty years ago when he lived and worked as a lawyer in downtown Charleston and had not yet discovered the peace of this cottage, located in a rural setting on Wadmalaw Island, South Carolina. A sea island once renowned for the silky texture of its cotton, which was exported to England before the Civil War, Wadmalaw lies only twenty minutes by car from downtown Charleston, but feels far more remote. "I told my malapropping real estate agent I was looking for something secluded," Trenholm says. "He called me back and said, 'I've found something so excluded, you won't believe it.'"

That secluded property was the last remains of an old farm at the water's edge with a converted cotton gin house. After a hurricane destroyed their house in the early twentieth century, the farming family moved into what had been the gin house and made it their home, gradually adding room after room in hodgepodge fashion. By the time Trenholm purchased the cottage, neglect and the elements had taken over, rusting through the tin roof and rotting some of the walls. But the beauty of the landscape—a nearby vacant field now returned to woodlands, an unkempt garden blooming with massive old camellias, and the embrace of the surrounding salt marsh—had endured, and he was captivated.

Trenholm Walker added this deck to the converted cotton gin house when
he transformed it into his country retreat. His wife, Susan Hull Walker, selected
throw pillows that bring together the colors of marsh grass, water, and sky.

Trenholm's goal for the first phase of renovation was to marry the house with its setting, opening up the interior spaces to the surrounding landscape with doors and windows, porches and decks. In a process he describes as the liberation of the house, the kitchen was redesigned to flow into the dining room, a deck was added overlooking the Wadmalaw Sound, an old sleeping porch was transformed into a screened living area, and a new sleeping porch that nestles in under the branches of live oak trees took shape above. "Whenever I'm up there, I feel like I've snuck out, like a kid escaping up a tree on a summer afternoon," says Trenholm of this last room.

In 1995, Trenholm's wife, Susan Hull Walker, moved from Charleston to Wadmalaw Island, where she fell in love with the land and met her future husband. While Trenholm's first energies had been focused upon renovating the house to embrace the landscape, Susan's attention was drawn to the landscape itself. "Some people think a Wadmalaw retreat is all about being on the water," she says. "But it's also about the country gardens, the paths, the camellias we've inherited." During the landscaping project, Susan discovered a circle of cedars in an overgrown part of the property: "I became enchanted with the possibility of planting a circular garden that could be an incubating place for me, out of which I could begin a new creative life."

Textiles such as a Turkish rug and kuba cloth from Africa (draped over a hand-hewn ladder) and rustic furnishings like a table from Guatemala with mismatched legs are reminders of Susan and Trenholm's travels.

At the time, Susan was studying the textile arts. She set up a studio in a barn overlooking the garden and began sewing, weaving, dyeing, and collecting textiles. On weekends, she and Trenholm continued their transformation of the landscape, creating an arbor out of a tangled mass of wisteria, defining paths and vistas through the trees, and cultivating a naturalistic garden of flowering trees, lush canna lilies, and hardy flowers. In a few years, they were married in the circle of cedars.

Soon afterward, the couple refocused on the house, continuing the process of transforming the ungainly structure into a commodious home at ease in its natural setting. "It was always a very simple, unpretentious place in the country," says Susan. "I wanted it to relax in its own skin and be just that." The house was also a place for the couple to relax in their skins and nurture their souls, whether by reading together, playing the piano, curling up by the fire, or lying beneath a ceiling fan on the sleeping porch. Combining her own artistic eye and love of textiles with the expertise of interior designer Gil Evans,

Opposite: *Pillows sewn from Guatemalan* huipiles *add bright notes of color to the dining room, while the house's sea island setting is invoked by a French mother-of-pearl pendant lamp, a Tanzanian basket with cowrie shells, and candleholders shaped like sea urchins.*

Right: *Whether traveling the world or just taking long walks on Wadmalaw Island and the nearby beaches, Susan and Trenholm are always picking up objects that please their eyes and delight their souls.*

Susan created an environment that is simultaneously sophisticated and rustic; exotic, yet rooted in a sense of place. "Rural places all over the world tend to give rise to a style that is close to the earth, with handmade items that are functional, but also beautiful. Primitive, rustic, yet global, reminding us of the places to which we've traveled—we wanted our surroundings to reflect this simple style," explains Susan.

The resulting décor includes rough-hewn tables from Guatemala, benches from Africa, and furniture from China, France, and the American South.

Handwoven, naturally dyed textiles draw these disparate objects together, uniting the many countries where Susan has studied with the history of Wadmalaw itself, where cotton and indigo were cultivated. In the guest room, for example, she has combined her great-aunt's quilt with a pillow covered in contemporary fabric made in Thailand and produced by her friend Eve Blossom, noting that their simplicity and earthy colors complement each other.

Whether sitting with friends on porch benches amply cushioned with pillows or working in the garden, Susan and Trenholm continually succumb to the spell of their island escape. They listen to the night sounds—dueling raccoons and possums, the slap of fish jumping in water, the throaty calls of herons. And they watch their fellow creatures. Susan describes a bald eagle fighting an osprey over prey. Trenholm muses over the solitary nobility of large wading birds. "I like being subject to tidal cycles," he says. "One moment, I'm looking upon flooded marsh, and the next, sculpted mud with a bird hunting along its edge. The landscape evolves every second of the day."

Curry-colored walls, a bed draped with paisley hangings, an ikat robe from Uzbekistan, and a length of sari silk evoke a mood of sensual and exotic escape in the master bedroom.

Coral, shells from nearby beaches, a spindle from Turkey, and a French farm table decorate the sleeping porch that Susan also uses as a writing room. A painting of the room made by friend Mclean Stith sits on the writing table.

Above: *Simple furniture painted white and handmade textiles, including a quilt made by Susan's great-aunt (thrown over a chair) and pillows of hand-loomed Thai silk, create a relaxed atmosphere in the guest room.*

Opposite: *Susan and Trenholm trained a massive wisteria vine over an arbor so that this outdoor dining area offers an environment of moist, cool shade on even the hottest days.*

Left: *French Art Deco chairs with colorful upholstered seats surround the dining room table set with vintage Fiestaware, cutlery with bakelite handles from the 1930s, and glasses that were sold as collectible peanut butter jars in the 1950s. A painted head that may have once been a bowsprit adorns a column.*

Above: *Jo Humphreys' collection of Fiestaware is displayed in a cabinet fronted with a pair of antique screen doors.*

little halfway

AN EARLY-TWENTIETH-CENTURY COTTAGE
IN THE HUNT COUNTRY

The Plains, Virginia ⸎

L ong before the word "fancy" came to be associated with the elegant, refined, and highly decorated, it meant fantasy. And that is the meaning Osborne Phinizy Mackie has in mind when he uses the word to describe the overall aesthetic of the cottage in Virginia's Hunt Country that he shares with Morgan Delaney. Filled with antiques and decorated with compositions of butterfly wings under glass and tinsel paintings (framed works of *verre églomisé* backed with foil), the cottage delights all who enter it. One recent houseguest, Bertrand du Vignaud, the president of the World Monuments Fund Europe, likened it to a charming Russian dacha nestled in the forest.

When Osborne and Morgan viewed the cottage for the first time thirteen years ago, it was merely a time-ravaged vestige of the simple country life that once characterized Fauquier County. A square bungalow-type dwelling with a hipped roof and backed by a barn, a henhouse, and a pair of privies (one for ladies, one for gents), it was constructed in the first years of the twentieth century as an unpretentious farmhouse. Although the county's landscape of rolling hills, extensive meadowland, and shady forest is better known as a riding and foxhunting retreat for residents of nearby Washington, D.C. and Alexandria, it has a much longer history as fertile farmland.

Tall evergreens dwarf the diminutive cottage that Morgan Delaney and Osborne Phinizy Mackie call their country home. Built in the early decades of the twentieth century, it is a simple bungalow with a hipped tin roof pierced by four dormers that provide light and ventilation for a second-story bedroom and bath.

and bathroom ceilings to expose rough-hewn beams. Then they began to infuse the rooms with elegance and character, hiring a friend, decorative painter Rachel Keebler, to faux grain doors and stipple walls to resemble the appearance of timeworn distemper paint. The doors, painted with an old-fashioned beer-based

A faux-grained door featuring the silhouette of a yawning man leads off the living room into the master bedroom. Within, even more extravagantly faux-grained furniture adds visual appeal.

medium, are not only exquisite facsimiles of mahogany graining, but also are replete with hidden jokes. Caricatures of Osborne and Morgan, a rabbit contemplating a carrot, a strutting cockerel—these are just a few of the pictorial elements she concealed amid the grain, taking some artistic license in the process. "I love visual tricks," says Osborne, speaking not only of the doors, but also the folk paintings on glass he collects. "Tinsel paintings have an innate sparkle. If you don't know what they are, you wonder, why are those paintings on glass so very bright? It's the tinsel, or foil backing, gleaming and sparkling so subtly, that adds the extra dimension."

In the dining room, an Eastlake screen in front of the fireplace provides further mysterious glimmer, with its many-hued tropical butterflies suspended between panes of antique glass. It seems to glow with an inner light, especially on cloudy days. While fitting in with the fanciful aesthetic informing the décor, this vibrant screen also pays homage to the large butterfly population that hovers around Little Halfway. "People come to see us and leave thinking this is the lepidopteran capital of Virginia," says Morgan, who also has hung framed antique compositions of butterfly wings under glass, some of which belonged to Osborne's great-grandmother, upon many walls of the little house.

Dignified southern furniture of the eighteenth and early nineteenth centuries, mostly made in Virginia and Maryland, adds ballast to the playful objects decorating the walls. "We agreed from the outset that this would not be a house for hand-me-downs not good enough for the house in town," Osborne says. The late-eighteenth-century Virginia dining table that

The cottage's pyramidal roof accommodates a comfortable bedroom furnished with early-nineteenth-century low-post beds from Pennsylvania and Caucasian rugs.

extends to seat twelve was already in the collection, but he notes, "it was hardly a hand-me-down." Because the rooms are small, the two often had to hunt far and wide for pieces that were the right scale.

One of their best finds is a cherry corner cupboard with a dramatically stepped cornice made in West Virginia in the early nineteenth century. Its height so closely matches that of the dining room's ceiling that Osborne and Morgan held their breath as they gently tipped it into the corner; it just squeezed in, with less than an inch to spare. Delicately mullioned glass doors reveal a collection of Wedgwood creamware befitting the most elegant English country house. American Aesthetic Movement frames hanging empty on the dining room wall await the arrival of two ornithological paintings commissioned from Robin Hill, a celebrated bird painter with a country place nearby. The finished works will depict hummingbirds on bee balm and indigo buntings on sumac—fauna and flora indigenous to the area.

Despite the elegance of these accoutrements, the interior retains a rustic mood imbued by the intimate proportions, Arts and Crafts–era light fixtures, grain-painted Victorian furniture in the bedrooms and bathroom, and an old-fashioned kitchen and porch. The regular visits of local wildlife, including rabbits, deer, foxes, wild turkeys, and even an occasional bear, emphasize the distance from the city. "Our original idea was to come to the country and simply rusticate," recalls Osborne. But country life has turned out to be far more sociable than the two ever imagined. "Fauquier County is filled with the most delightful people you'll ever meet," exclaims Osborne. "We lead a wonderful life with warm friends in a setting that charms all the senses."

crystal creek

A 1939 LOG CABIN IN THE BLUE RIDGE FOOTHILLS

Roanoke Valley, Virginia ⮑

Not long ago, a friend telephoned Lucy Tkachenko at her cabin in Roanoke Valley late in the evening and asked if she could bring someone over for a visit. In answer to Lucy's protests about the hour, her friend said, "I've told her how magical your place is. Can I please, please bring her?" Lucy relented, and the three sat on the porch of her tiny log cabin, which hangs on the edge of a creek bank beneath which mountain waters cascade. When a luna moth landed on the porch rail, the visitor stared at its large silky wings striped with green and asked, "What is it?" "It's the creek fairy," Lucy replied. Since then, sightings of and stories about the creek fairy have abounded —and with good reason. Even if the creek fairy is just a figment of Lucy's imagination, there is no denying the fact that her home and its setting are utterly enchanting. "I happen to think my place is a little bit magical," says Lucy.

Lucy, whose avocations include working at a luxury car dealership, styling displays for a Roanoke home boutique called Present Thyme, and making jewelry, had been making regular visits to her sister in Virginia for years while raising her family in Richmond, and later Canada. During one such trip, the two drove along Crystal Creek Road, a perilously winding drive that runs along a

Lucy Tkachenko's cabin is among the rustic hunting and fishing camp residences that cropped up in the 1930s and 1940s along Roanoke Valley's Crystal Creek Road. These simple houses were constructed of readily available materials: logs, river rocks, and wood salvaged from railroad boxcars.

creek in Roanoke Valley. They stopped to see friends who lived in a cabin on the creek, and Lucy told her sister, "If you can get me that cabin, I'll move here." Lucy returned to Canada, but the cabin on the creek remained lodged in her memory, and a few years later when her grown children left home and her marriage ended, she came back to Crystal Creek Road and asked the owners if they would sell it. They declined, but another cabin nearby was available for sale, and Lucy bought it on the spot.

Lucy's cabin is constructed in a rustic style popular in the area in the 1930s and 1940s, when single men or families built simple fishing and hunting camps in the undeveloped countryside. Logs chinked with mortar give the cabins their characteristic striped appearance, and stone chimneys and foundations offer rugged texture. Crystal Creek Road was originally a logging road, along which timber farmers would haul wood to the railroad terminus in Roanoke. Thus, logs and river rocks were easily accessible building materials, and beams and planks salvaged from railroad boxcars offered another inexpensive source of wood. Lucy's house contains all three materials, including a piece of boxcar plank inscribed "Built by R. E. Sutherland, September 1939." The cabin almost seems to rise up out of the creek bank on its tall stone foundation. The dark brown log walls, with their creamy striations of mortar, blend into the sylvan setting like a well-camouflaged bird. When viewed from creek level, only the white porch railing stands out clearly to distinguish this as a dwelling place among the local flora. But drawing nearer, the sight of

Opposite: *Lucy replaced an ugly metal porch railing with a wooden one that adds charm to the façade. Frequent excursions to yard sales, the local Goodwill thrift store, and a nearby flea market named Happy's have yielded the porch's fanciful collection of furniture and decorative objects.*

Above: *An informal garden of daylilies and hostas provide summer-long blooms in terraced beds bounded by retaining walls. The walls were made from rocks taken from the creek below.*

cheerful red cushions on rocking chairs and benches, and signs reading "Live Bait" and "Dream with a View," make it clear that someone lives within.

Approaching the cabin, you might hear a voice as creaking and shrill as a fairytale witch's crying: "Beautiful Bella, you're so beautiful, Bella." A peek into one of the windows reveals its source: a chartreuse parrot with a red-and-yellow beak and an extensive vocabulary. Just one glimpse of the interior is enough to enchant any visitor as completely as it did when Lucy first saw the cottage. Since her initial visit, however, Lucy has remodeled the interior and decorated extensively, drawing upon her talents as an artist and stylist and her passion as a flea market habitué and salvager. What she initially imagined to be just a two- or three-week project became a six-month-long undertaking when she decided to reconfigure the small, dark rooms sheltered within the cabin's walls. She removed the ceiling in the living room, revealing rafters salvaged from boxcars. A canoe she discovered in the local Goodwill thrift store perches high above the room on the rafters. At eye level, a mantel that Lucy contrived from salvaged architectural elements lends charm to a rough stone fireplace. She also put in stairs designed from more salvaged materials that lead to a bedroom loft overlooking the living room.

Continuing her effort to create an airier, more spacious feel, Lucy removed a wall that separated the kitchen from the living room. She designed a countertop island to divide the rooms instead, and covered its sides with pressed-tin ceiling panels found at a demolition site in Roanoke. "I'm not opposed to stopping and going through people's trash," she laughs,

Opposite: *A soaring living space was created by removing the ceiling of the main room to expose rafters and roof trusses. Salvaged elements from an old staircase lead to a sleeping loft. A chalkware lamp on the far table is another find from Lucy's salvaging and shopping expeditions.*

Above: *Lucy decorated the plain stone fireplace with columns and a mantelpiece that she bought separately. The painting of a fairy was a gift from her sister, who purchased it at Present Thyme, a home furnishings boutique in Roanoke where Lucy creates displays.*

The cabin's original bathing facilities were limited to a small shower. Lucy transformed one of the small bedrooms into a charming bathroom, where more of the pressed-tin decorative panels add a feminine element of texture and pattern to the rustic log surfaces.

confessing a habit that clearly renders decorative treasure. She used more of the pressed-tin panels to decorate the exterior of a whirlpool tub she installed in a bathroom created from one of the cabin's two tiny bedrooms.

The parrot, Bella, spends the night in an enclosed sleeping porch on the far side of the kitchen, which also doubles as Lucy's dining room. The mistress of the house slumbers in a sumptuous bed beneath a window overlooking the creek. Saints gaze over the bed from a mural that once graced a church wall, and the sound of the creek provides a constant, lulling soundtrack. "I always sleep with the window open so I can hear the creek," says Lucy. She recalls waking up one winter night to the sound of splashing. When she looked out the window, she saw everything covered with snow and a deer drinking in the middle of the creek.

The cabin's setting abounds with wildlife. The creek is home to an ever-growing family of ducks that swim and play in the waters year-round, as well as a great blue heron that some neighbors swear has been a regular visitor for forty years. Lucy first spied the majestic bird sitting on a boulder in the creek on a rainy spring day: "When she swoops into the air, she is a gorgeous sight to behold." The property is also home to a toad that has shown up three years in a row in the same spot of ivy-covered rocks. Friends have suggested that Lucy try kissing it, to see what might happen. While she hasn't tried that particular bit of magic yet, she does know that dreams do come true—as evidenced by this tiny house in the mountains with a porch on a creek.

An ecclesiastical mural with the otherworldly air of a
Russian icon contrasts with the earthy sensuality of Lucy's
bed, which is made up with Bella Notte linens. Lucy always
sleeps with the window open so that she can listen to the
ever-changing voice of the creek that flows beneath it.

summer rhythms

A COMPOUND OF NINETEENTH- AND EARLY-TWENTIETH-CENTURY DWELLINGS

Flat Rock, North Carolina ⚉

This family from Charleston, South Carolina, has been summering in Flat Rock for generations. A network of parents, children, and grandchildren, as well as uncles, aunts, and cousins share numerous houses perched upon the North Carolina hills with green vistas, in shady glades, and along cool waters. Each house has its own family nucleus that follows its own daily rhythm of meals and activities, but they are all connected in a larger whole—like a quilt made out of individually sewn and patterned squares.

In 1961, a new element was introduced into the composition when a young son brought his British bride back home to enjoy the last ripe days of summer with his family following their honeymoon in Europe. "It was landlocked, and raining, and September, and there wasn't anybody here but the ancients," she says, and remembers thinking gloomily, "We are going to spend every summer here." Forty-five years later and now the matriarch of her own family, she is still coming to Flat Rock each year. "And I love it dearly," she says. Among her blessings, she numbers the fact that her three sons have married women who love Flat Rock as much as she does. The family compound has

A pair of chimneys and white porch pillars topped with a Chippendale-style balustrade add symmetry and elegance to the 1934 cottage that is the compound's main house.

grown as a result. Though her first husband died more than a decade ago, the homeowner continues to spend every summer in Flat Rock. She is joined now by her second husband, an architect from Boston, who has become a Flat Rock convert as well.

In the beginning, the homeowner and her first husband spent the summer months in a large 1934 cottage presided over by her mother-in-law. When the couple's sons were small, they purchased a farmhouse known as the Pace Place, located on the far side of a cow pasture from the family cottage. Built in 1880 or 1890, it was suffering from advanced decrepitude, but its impeccable siting and country charm were irresistible. "Country people just know how to do the bend in the road; how to place the house in the corner of a field; how to face it north so that there is summer shade on the porch," she says.

With the help of their three young boys and their caretaker, the young family set about shoring up the house's sagging ceiling with beams made from trees

cut on the property. They removed a wall separating the first floor's two main rooms to create a large great room divided by an original double-sided fireplace. With their children's assistance, they put a fresh coat of paint on the pine floors, applied new cedar paneling to the walls, and repaired and replaced old beadboard paneling in other parts of the house. When the project was complete, the house was not only structurally sound, but a good bit more commodious, with a master bedroom, bathroom, and kitchen on the ground floor and three bedrooms upstairs.

When they acquired the little red farmhouse, it had no electricity or plumbing. After toying with the idea of keeping it that way, they succumbed to the convenience of modern technology. Then they set about decorating it in a comfortable style with furniture purchased from flea markets and yard sales, family artwork, and textiles collected locally and abroad. The latter range from hand-crocheted lace placemats to richly colored kilims bought in Turkey. A pair of metal beds painted blue offer simple sleeping arrangements in one of the second-floor children's rooms and a fine old locally made four-poster bed graces the master bedroom.

Left: *Several hundred boxwood trees were planted in a spiraling maze on the edge of the cow pasture in a unique way to mark the millennium.*

Opposite: *Old wicker furniture, a metal glider draped with an embroidered textile from Turkey, and a Turkish kilim contribute comfort and style to the cottage's broad porch— a favorite gathering space for reading, playing cards, and enjoying refreshing drinks.*

For more than a decade, the family summered at the Pace Place, gathering daily at the large main cottage across the pasture for meals and parties. When the present homeowner inherited this cottage, she passed the little red farmhouse on to one of her sons and his wife, who now enjoy it with their two children. The two other sons and their wives swell the ranks each summer, living in the former servant's quarters of the main house and another nearby cottage, formerly owned by a great-grandmother.

The new generation in residence at the Pace Place has gradually made changes of their own, lightening its wood-paneled rooms with soft shades of blue and green that complement the summer landscape. "One room was so dark that the children were afraid to sleep in it," says the present resident, who brightened it with white-painted furniture and headboards. She painted her own bedroom a shade of pale green inspired by a pink-and-green quilt found in a local antiques store.

Every few years witnesses the addition of new family members and new structures or amenities. In celebration of the millennium, the family planted a maze of boxwood on the edge of the cow pasture. With three architects in the family, discussion swelled on the subject of the maze's design, yet on the day the boxwoods arrived, no final plan had been chosen. "There we were one morning drinking our coffee and chatting, some of us still in our dressing gowns, and these trucks drove into the fields and the boxwoods began to be unloaded," the homeowner remembers. "We all got out there and just started arranging them."

Opposite: *The residents designed this circular dining pavilion supported by posts made from locust trees grown on the property. Sited on a natural rise of land above a cow pasture, the pavilion captures breezes for delightfully cool summer lunches or dinners.*

Above: *A large screened porch addition doubles the size of this modest servants' quarters constructed in the 1930s.*

The result is a serene composition of interconnected spirals replete with blind corners and dead-ends. Each year the boxwoods grow taller, and the maze becomes more difficult to travel.

Two years ago, the homeowner and her husband built a dining pavilion on a natural terrace overlooking the pasture and the maze. With a wood shingle roof supported by locust posts cut on the property, the circular structure provides an outdoor dining area that can seat anywhere from four to twenty-four, depending on the number of families in residence and visiting friends. The family recently hosted a large party during which the pavilion became a bandstand; local musicians serenaded the guests, who dined at tables scattered on the lawn.

The newest addition to the family's gathering places is a summer living and dining room added to the former servants' quarters next to the main house. The large screened porch doubles the dwelling's size, creating an airy spot to gather for drinks or meals. Another son and his wife, who use this cottage during visits from London, designed a long table that easily seats twelve from several old pine boards that had been stored in the root cellar of the Pace Place for years. The family also enlarged the utility porch opening off the kitchen of the main house to serve as another breezy dining spot, or to accommodate buffet-style serving of meals enjoyed elsewhere on the property.

One of the family's favorite moments of the day is when the horses and cows in the pasture come up to the fence just beyond the back porch of the Pace Place in their cycle of grazing. It seems almost as if they, too, want to participate in the family's rotation of gatherings throughout the days and weeks, drawing close to the farmhouse at one time, then to the maze and the dining pavilion at another. Throughout the day, the cattle's lowing echoes across the fields, yet another reminder of the timeless rhythms that connect this family to one another, to generations past, and to this place in the country.

A locally made hand-crocheted canopy adds elegance to the simple, painted furniture of the guest quarters' bedroom.

Left: *Light-colored upholstery, painted floors, and a masonry fireplace offer pale contrast to the great room's richly burnished cedar paneling and wooden beams.*

Above: *Miscellaneous objects found on the property, preserved flora and fauna, coins, shells, toys and other items are stored and catalogued in a tiny outbuilding the family calls the children's museum.*

remote retreat

A 1930S RURAL COTTAGE

Johns Island, South Carolina ⟞⟞

Since as far back as the nineteenth century, many Charleston families have owned three places: a house in town, a cottage at the beach or in the mountains to escape the heat and diseases of summer, and a rustic country getaway for hunting and fishing. Rural real estate was not expensive back then, so having two or three residences was not a sign of great affluence. In the days when a mosquito bite could cause a life-threatening fever (although at the time it was thought that bad summer air was the culprit), escaping from the muggy city was more a necessity than a luxury. Although visits to a country getaway might bear tangible fruit in the form of racks of venison, braces of wild turkey or quail, or baskets full of fish and shellfish, the main purpose of these rural retreats was just that: retreat.

The simple two-room cottage on Johns Island owned by author Josephine Humphreys and her husband, Tom Hutcheson, is a classic example. The drive to the cottage takes less than forty-five minutes from downtown Charleston, but as the road crosses over several bridges connecting increasingly rural islands, the landscape gradually shifts from urban to suburban to farmland. The last mile of the road is unpaved, passing through flat tomato fields shaded here and there by giant

Fluted Doric columns salvaged from a house in downtown Charleston replace the original four-by-four-inch pillars that once propped up the porch, giving this simple cottage a classical appearance despite its small size and humble materials.

Above: *The shutters are painted "ha'nt" blue, a color that in Gullah tradition is believed to deter supernatural beings from entering a house. A perforated basket-weave pattern decorates the seats and backs of the metal porch chairs, offering stylish ventilation for cool outdoor seating.*

Opposite: *The cottage's walls are covered with beaded pine panels painted white. A cutout between the kitchen and living room improves the flow of light and air. Large jugs of fermenting wine are a common sight on the kitchen floor.*

live oak trees. The private driveway to the cottage winds through a large stand of such trees that cast cool shadows and an amber carpet of leaves upon the ground. It ends beside a little white house with shutters painted "ha'nt" blue (in Gullah tradition, a hue thought to repel troublesome supernatural beings called "ha'nts" or "haints") that looks like it has been there forever.

According to Tom and Jo, who bought the house from Jo's father, it was built in the 1930s and owned by a physician who worked for the railroad. There are vestiges of several much older buildings on the property, including a Freedmen's Bureau school for former slaves and their descendents. The doctor lived in a nearby town and frequented the cottage as a weekend retreat. When he retired, the railroad company gave him the train bell that is mounted on a stanchion outside.

When Jo's father bought the property, she recalls that the cottage "was not really considered livable. Daddy never spent the night there, but he loved the place." Jo and her sisters spent time there crabbing, fishing, and shrimping; she even remembers hunting expeditions: "Daddy hunted ducks, and I remember he took me on a rabbit hunt when I shot my first, and my last, rabbit."

Despite the fact that the cottage was so rustic ("a nice way to put it," Jo interjects), she and her husband moved into the tiny dwelling for a year when her father offered it to them rent-free upon Tom's graduation from law school. The walls were flimsy and there

was no heat, but Jo says "we didn't care how cold it was, rent-free is never too cold." That year, the couple found themselves living much closer to nature than they anticipated. Snakes, mice, bugs, and lizards made themselves at home in the cottage, and animals outside would chew on the wood and try to get in. "I imagine that if you could actually see what was going on out there at night, you'd be just shocked," says Jo. "In my imagination, I see hundreds of raccoons, possums,

Opposite: *Freshly picked produce from the garden airs in the sink, below shelves filled with canned vegetables from last year's crop. A tiny painting that Jo made of the house decorates the wall above a corkboard constructed of old wine corks.*

Above: *The living room is furnished with simple painted furniture and folk art. The painting of a spot-tail bass tailing (showing its tail above the water) was done by a friend, Terry Hamlin, on a piece of old clapboard from a renovation project.*

Below: *Tom's mother made the rag rugs that decorate the cottage's floors. Although the colors have faded over time, they still brighten the rooms.*

Above: *In the bedroom, a tangle of jasmine vine, bright with yellow blossoms, brightens the top of a nineteenth-century chest of drawers in the American Empire style.*

Opposite: *A brilliant chenille bedspread depicting peacocks draws the eye in the bedroom, its bright pattern echoed in the rag rugs covering the floor. The plain furnishings include a 1930s metal bed, simple bedside tables, and a painted trunk.*

alligators, deer, otter, foxes, bobcats." In fact, they have seen all those animals among the area's abundant wildlife, as well as numerous birds, including barn owls, screech owls, great horned owls, and chuck will's widows.

While Jo's impressions of the house hang somewhere between a shudderingly sublime appreciation of nature, red in tooth and claw, and idyllic childhood memories (which she is now recreating for her grandchildren), Tom's approach is more that of a Jeffersonian architect-gardener-philosopher, with a touch of Swiss Family Robinson zeal. Semiretired from practicing law, Tom spends many days and nights at the cottage throughout the year, where he divides his time between gardening, fishing, reading, and shoring up the structures. He has fully restored the house, removing a porch enclosure, replacing clapboard siding and interior walls, and rebuilding the front porch.

For this last project, Tom used four fluted Doric columns salvaged from a downtown house as props while preparing to replace the original four-by-four inch pillars. "I put them up there with tongue in cheek, and everybody liked them," he says. So the columns remained, lending the cottage a bit more elegance than it had known in previous incarnations.

Within, the cottage has two main rooms clad in white-painted pine paneling and arranged side by side beneath the gabled roof. A wood-burning stove, the only source of heat, sits on the brick hearth of a fireplace set in the gable side of the living room. Simple

A small vineyard planted with a variety of muscadine grapes, including sweet scuppernongs, yields dozens of bottles of Tom's homemade wine each year.

homemade furniture lines the walls, mixed in with a few bought pieces including a drop-leaf table painted the same blue as the house's shutters and a trio of spindle-back chairs. Jo snapped the chairs up at a roadside flea market moments before an interior decorator made a bid for them. "I love them because they look so delicate for kitchen chairs . . . almost French," says Jo. A navigational chart showing the waters that flow just outside the cottage, where the Stono and Kiawah rivers meet to form the Stono Inlet, hangs above the table. A Haitian painting depicting the wedding of a minor Haitian dignitary adorns the opposite wall, placed there when Jo's niece spent her wedding night at the house.

The bedroom features a simple metal bed from the 1930s, one of several that Jo has collected: "As I understand it, when you bought a mattress back then, you'd get a bed like this for free, or maybe you had to pay five dollars." Jo likes their simple decoration and sturdy design. It provides the perfect foil for an outrageously gaudy chenille bedspread depicting a pair of bright blue peacocks preening on a scarlet field. The American Empire–style dresser inherited from Tom's grandfather lends a more dignified note. Throughout the house, rag rugs made by Tom's mother create bright pools of color against a floor of gray-painted heart pine boards.

The kitchen is diminutive but quite functional, with a large enameled sink and open shelves holding an array of country-style condiments, including cane syrup, home-canned pickles, and a selection of barbecue rubs. On the floor, several large jugs of homemade wine emit the occasional bubble as they ferment, revealing another of Tom's favorite country pastimes.

After the couple bought the house, Tom and his father-in-law William Humphreys planted a small vineyard of muscadine grapes. Long interested in making wines, William had sought advice from Lester Hemingway, the famous writer's brother and author of *Drink It Yourself*, a pamphlet, Jo explains, "about how to make wine out of just about anything, including potatoes and grass." Tom has since expanded the vineyard to include seventy-two vines and makes ten to sixty gallons of wine each year (depending upon variables like rain and raccoons) from several types of muscadines, such as succulent scuppernongs. He has also constructed a small greenhouse, where he cultivates a variety of plants, and prepared a fenced plot that now yields tomatoes, lettuces, herbs, and other vegetables and fruit. When he's not working on the house or the nearby pole barn (a pair of corrugated metal shed roofs supported by poles), Tom goes fishing. "There's a lot of fish, shrimp, crabs, and oysters out there. We catch spot-tail bass, trout, and croakers," he says, listing the boundless fruits of the sea.

One of the couple's two grown sons, Allen, likes to collect oysters from the creeks, which he then steams under burlap sacks in a freestanding brick fireplace, a vestige of an old caretaker's house next to the cottage. Steamed oysters are a highlight at the annual post-Thanksgiving party that the family throws, which also usually includes a whole pig cooked the old-fashioned way, in a pit. In inclement weather, picnicking takes place in the barn, otherwise on the ruins of the caretaker's house or in Helen's House, a brightly painted, irregularly shaped pavilion perched on a creek bank.

Although it is painted bright Caribbean tones, the shape of Helen's House reminds Jo of abandoned roadside shacks in the rural South. It was created as a set for the filming of her novel, *Rich in Love*, in which a wife and mother of two daughters runs away from home to find solitude in an abandoned house. When the filming was over, Jo bought it and had it moved to Johns Island. Aside from making a great picnic house, Jo likes to go there to read or simply to look out over the creek banks and marshes that bristle with spartina, a grass that turns luminous chartreuse in summer. From Helen's House, she watches for porpoises that swim up into the creeks and the many birds that hover above the waters and the thickets of trees. "It's a very remote place for how unremote it is," says Tom.

Built as a set for the filming of her novel, Rich in Love, *and painted in bright Caribbean hues, Jo bought this structure and had it moved to the Johns Island property.*

Left: *Vintage wicker furniture and painted trunks offer durable and comfortable seating for relaxed gatherings on the main cabin's porch, which can be warmed by a roaring fire on chilly autumn days and nights.*

Above: *A staircase sheltered with a gabled roof of cedar shingles links the two cabins housing the master bedroom and the living areas.*

Above: *In the guest bedroom, American antiques complement the country-style surfaces of old chinked logs and planks covered with milk paint.*

Opposite: *Nineteen-thirties chairs with white upholstery inject a modern note in the living area adjacent to the kitchen, where an antique Oushak carpet offers a touch of luxury underfoot.*

Cushioned wicker furniture provides comfortable seating around the hearth. A window placed high in the porch's gable brings more light to this breezy living space, where a floor painted barn red contrasts with the surrounding green foliage.

An outdoor staircase, open on the sides and sheltered by gabled roofs, connects the central cabin to a second one that houses the master bedroom suite. While the communal gathering spaces are decorated in a palette of hearty reds and oranges, for this serene retreat Charleston-based interior designer Amelia Handegan selected cool shades of lavender, white, gray, and brown. In contrast to the room's rugged setting of chinked wood and stone, Handegan floated yards of sheer white netting over a reproduction campaign bed of silvery metal to create a romantic centerpiece. A white bedspread with a deep hem of crocheted lace adds another feminine note to the masculine setting, as do long curtains and throw pillows of lavender silk. A pair of leather-clad French Art Deco club chairs provides stylish seating around the fireplace, contrasting with primitive wooden tables and stools. The owner selected the charming nineteenth-century French painting depicting the Saint of Charity, who gazes calmly from above the fireplace. The master bath offers an equally delightful blend of the masculine and feminine, the rustic and refined, with its porcelain bathtub and primitive pine furnishings. A porch for two completes the cabin's accommodations. Paralleling the bedroom, it provides the perfect spot for afternoon naps on an old iron daybed, cushioned in ticking and dressed up with silk pillows. Wicker chairs on the opposite end are ideal for quiet tête-a-têtes or savoring morning coffee.

With four children ranging in age from fourteen to twenty-four, as well as many friends who like to visit, the owners made sure there was plenty of space for family members and guests. In fact, they devoted a whole separate house to them: a two-story cabin just a short walk from the other structures. This cabin boasts two double bedrooms, a small sitting area, a kitchenette, and a porch on the ground floor. In addition, a bunk room above sleeps five. Each twin bed nestles in its own curtained alcove in this most ingeniously designed room that is perfect for occasions when the whole family—or several families—gather at the property.

Throughout the cabins, Greene and Handegan have complemented the original building materials with recycled barn boards and antique French oak used for the floors, wall surfaces, and cabinetry. Where paint was needed to add color, Handegan selected milk paint, which has a matte, chalky finish more appropriate in this setting than a glossy look. For the furnishings, she mixed eclectic antiques from England, France, and the United States. Whimsical chandeliers designed from antlers and lamps of forged iron contribute to the rustic mood. The owner gives credit to Handegan for creating an exceptional interior: "Her eclectic style brought a sense of luxury and comfort that really makes the cabin special."

Opposite: *Jute curtains suspended on rods fashioned from branches and a cotton rag rug on the floor maintain a natural palette of colors and textures in the sleeping loft.*

Right: *A metal daybed creates a perfect spot to take in the view on a porch opening off the master bedroom.*

The creative interiors match the imaginative exterior details designed by Greene. "Tim really has a great knack for that mountain feel," says the owner, who admires the bark siding, stone fireplaces, and other architectural details that are at once appropriate and unconventional. "He has an excellent sense of proportion, so everything he does seems to fit."

ACKNOWLEDGMENTS ~

This book is the result of the contributions of many people who shared with me their cottages, their information and expertise, their connections, and their hospitality.

In addition to thanking my editor, Sandy Gilbert, for her patience and guidance, my publisher, Charles Miers, for his faith in my work, and my graphic designer, Eric Mueller, for his brilliant design, I would also like to thank the following for their invaluable assistance:

Meg Campbell

The Cavalier, Virginia Beach, Virginia

Flo Fahrbach

George Gattoni

Michael Haga

Julie Howard

Paula Illingworth

Ann Jones

Ellen Kiser

Laura Miller

Ocracoke Preservation Society, North Carolina

Professional Color, Metairie, Louisiana

Scott and Leslie Provow

Quill Ruffner

Lynn Scrabis

Feilding Tyler

The WaterColor Inn, Florida

WaterColor Resort, Florida

Joyce and Rod Wilson

Opposite: *The rising sun illuminates the mountainous horizon long before it brightens the lawn that slopes from the Cornwells' cottage and garden down to the misty lake.*

The following is a list of many of the interior designers and decorators, shops, and manufacturers whose products are featured in this book. The title of the chapter associated with each entry, and when appropriate, further identifying details, are noted after the name.

interior designers and decorators

JANE COSLICK
(project director and designer, *Tybee Time* and *Palm Cottage*)
Tybee Island, Georgia
(877) 524-9819
www.janecoslickcottages.com

GEORGE DAVIS
(*Island Harmony*)
Geo. P. Davis, Inc.
Nantucket Island, Massachusetts
(508) 228-5200
www.weeds-nantucket.com

RUTH EDWARDS ANTIQUES
& INTERIORS
(*A Fish Tale*)
Hilton Head, South Carolina
(843) 671-2223

GIL EVANS
(*Evolving Landscape*)
New York, New York
(843) 209-8857

AMELIA T. HANDEGAN, INC.
(*A Cabin of One's Own* and *Spirit House*)
Charleston, South Carolina
(843) 722-9373

ALLISON HILLIS, ABGD, INC.
(*Endless Summer*)
Atlantic Beach, Florida
(904) 249-4133

KATHLEEN HINES,
KMH DESIGN, INC.
(*Endless Summer*)
Jacksonville, Florida
(904) 519-9555
www.kmhdesigninc.com

JACQUELYNNE P. LANHAM
DESIGNS, INC.
(*Abiding Style*)
Atlanta, Georgia
(404) 364-0472

architects

TIM GREENE & ASSOCIATES
(*A Cabin of One's Own*)
Cashiers, North Carolina
(828) 743-2968

KAREN RUTTER, ACANTHUS
ARCHITECTS
(*Endless Summer*)
Jacksonville, Florida
(904) 241-4787

RICHARD SKINNER & ASSOCIATES
(*Abiding Style*)
Jacksonville, Florida
(904) 387-6710
www.rs-architects.com

JIM STRICKLAND, HISTORICAL
CONCEPTS
(*A Fish Tale*)
Peachtree City, Georgia
(770) 487-8041
www.historicalconcepts.com

resorts and communities

WaterColor, Florida
(*A Fish Tale*)
www.watercolor-vacations.com

WaterColor Inn
(*A Fish Tale*)
34 Goldenrod Circle
Santa Rosa Beach, Florida
(850) 534-5000
www.watercolorinn.com

furniture, lighting, and decorating details

Carolina Lowcountry Collection
Historic Charleston Foundation
Charleston, South Carolina
(800) 434-3186
www.historiccharleston.org

Dearing Antiques
(antique furniture, *A Cabin of One's Own*)
Atlanta, Georgia
(404) 233-6333

English Patina
(antique furniture, *A Cabin of One's Own*)
Charleston, South Carolina
(843) 762-2111

Estes Antiques
(pottery plates, and goblets, *Abiding Style*)
Cashiers, North Carolina
(828) 743-5623

Willis Everett
(antique heart pine, *A Fish Tale*)
Gay, Georgia
(706) 538-0180

Amelia T. Handegan Showroom
(furniture, artwork, and lighting, *A Cabin of One's Own* and *Spirit House*)
Charleston, South Carolina
(843) 722-9373

Hibernia Handmade
(pottery bowls, *Abiding Style*)
Neptune Beach, Florida
(904) 249-7321
www.hiberniahandmade.com

Holly Hunt
(contemporary candelabra, *Island Harmony* and *Abiding Style*)
www.hollyhunt.com

Hunter Fan Company
(ceiling fans, *A Cabin of One's Own*)
www.hunterfan.com

Johnson Lighting
(living room lighting, *Tybee Time*)
Savannah, Georgia
(912) 355-3852

Mainly Baskets
(family room chairs, *Abiding Style*)
www.mainlybaskets.com

Nierman Weeks
(steel campaign bed, *A Cabin of One's Own*)
(410) 923-0123

Page's Thieves Market
(vintage furniture and decorative objects, *Old Island Style*)
Mount Pleasant, South Carolina
(843) 884-9672

Paris Flea Market
(vintage furnishings and oyster shell pendant lamp, *Tybee Time*)
Savannah, Georgia
(912) 232-1500

Eloise Pickard
(vintage lighting, *A Fish Tale*)
Adairsville, Georgia
(404) 252-3244

PRESENT THYME
(bedding and art, *Crystal Creek*)
Roanoke, Virginia
(540) 342-9706
www.presentthyme.com

RYAN & BOYLE ANTIQUES
(antique furniture, *Summer Rhythms*)
Saluda, North Carolina
(828) 749-9790

SCOTT ANTIQUE MARKET
(antique and vintage furniture,
A Fish Tale)
Atlanta, Georgia
(404) 361-2000
www.scottantiquemarket.com

THE STALLS
(antique furniture, *A Cabin of
One's Own*)
Atlanta, Georgia
(404) 352-4430

TECNOSEDIA
(contemporary chairs and sofa,
Endless Summer)
Atlanta, Georgia
(404) 810-9081
www.tecnosedia.net

VILLAGE CRAFTSMEN
(furniture and decorative objects,
Past Present)
Ocracoke Island, North Carolina
(252) 928-5541
www.villagecraftsmen.com

VILLAGE GREEN ANTIQUE MALL
(antique furniture, *Summer Rhythms*)
Henderson, North Carolina
(828) 692-9057

WEDGWOOD
(Nantucket Basket china,
Island Harmony)
www.wedgwood.com or
www.weeds-nantucket.com

WEEDS
(antiques and decorative objects,
Island Harmony)
Nantucket Island, Massachusetts
(866) 559-3337
www.weeds-nantucket.com

TOBY WEST, LTD.
(antler lighting, *A Cabin of
One's Own*)
Atlanta, Georgia
(404) 233-7425

textiles and carpets

MURIEL BRANDOLINI
(batik print pillows, *Endless Summer*)
New York, New York
(212) 249-4920
www.murielbrandolini.com

DONGHIA
(turtle-patterned textiles,
Island Harmony)
www.donghia.com

FOAM AND FABRICS OUTLET
(fabrics, *Little Charleston of the
Mountains* and *Summer Rhythms*)
Fletcher, North Carolina
(828) 684-0801

VICTORIA HAGAN HOME
(blue and white fabric in double guest
room, *Abiding Style*)
New York, New York
(212) 888-3241
www.victoriahaganhome.com

LES INDIENNES
(bed hangings, *Evolving Landscape*)
Tuscon, Arizona
(520) 881-8122
www.lesindiennes.com

LULAN ARTISANS
(silk cushions and throws,
Evolving Landscape)
Charleston, South Carolina
(843) 722-0118
www.lulan.com

RUGS & TREASURES
(carpets, *A Cabin of One's Own*)
Atlanta, Georgia
(404) 812-1881

RUGS BY ROBINSON
(living room carpet, *Endless Summer*)
Atlanta, Georgia
(404) 364-9042

ZINN RUG GALLERY
(rugs, *Evolving Landscape*)
Charleston, South Carolina
(843) 577-0300
www.zinnruggallery.com

artwork

HAIDEE BECKER
(painting over fireplace, *A Cabin of One's Own*)
Represented by Timothy Tew Gallery
Atlanta, Georgia
(404) 869-0511

JOHN BUCK
(pastel in dining room, *Endless Summer*)
Represented by J. Johnson Gallery
Jacksonville Beach, Florida
(904) 435-3200

MARTY WHALEY ADAMS CORNWELL
(paintings, *Little Charleston of the Mountains*)
Represented by Wells Gallery
Charleston, South Carolina
(843) 853-3233
www.wellsgallery.com

ROBERT FLYNN
(palm tree paintings, *Endless Summer*)
Available from Allison Hillis
Jacksonville, Florida
(904) 249-4133

KAT HASTIE
(painting in dining room, *Evolving Landscape*)
(843) 577-0006
www.kathastie.com

ROBIN HILL
(ornithological paintings, *Little Halfway*)
Georgetown, Washington, D.C.
(202) 338-2878
www.robinhillartist.com

RACHEL KEEBLER
(decorative painting, *Little Halfway*)
White Lake, New York
(845) 583-7025
www.cobaltstudios.net

BELLAMY MURPHY
(paintings, *Tybee Time*)
Tybee Island, Georgia
(912) 786-8786

MCLEAN STITH
(painting on sleeping porch, *Evolving Landscape*)
Charleston, South Carolina
(843) 442-6832
mstith@bellsouth.net

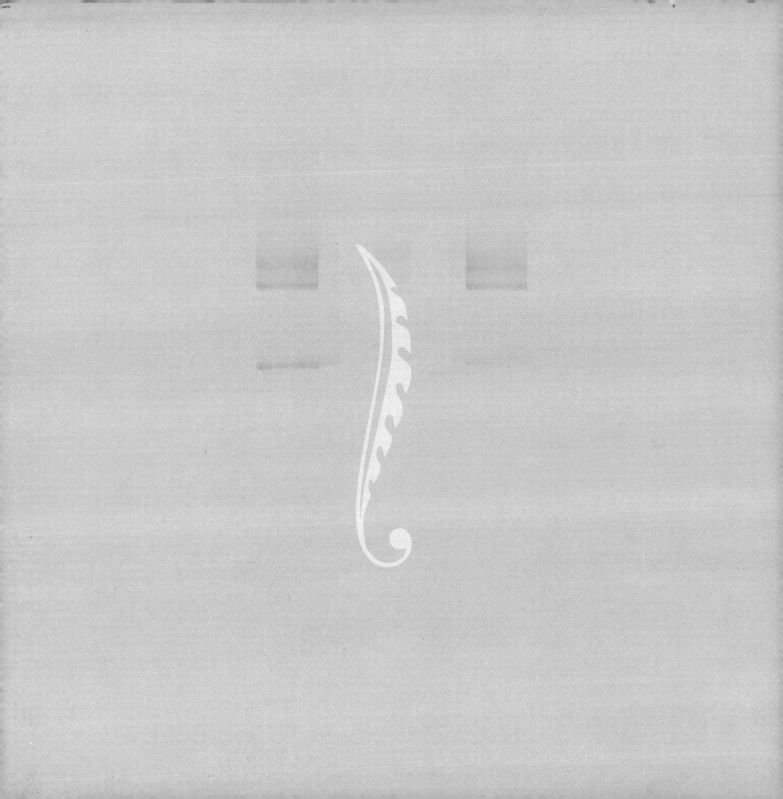